LIES

WE TELL
OURSELVES

GREG LAURIE

Regal

From Gospel Light
Ventura, California, U.S.A.

PUBLISHED BY REGAL BOOKS
FROM GOSPEL LIGHT
VENTURA, CALIFORNIA, U.S.A.
PRINTED IN THE U.S.A.

Regal

Regal Books is a ministry of Gospel Light, a Christian publisher dedicated to serving the local church. We believe God's vision for Gospel Light is to provide church leaders with biblical, user-friendly materials that will help them evangelize, disciple and minister to children, youth and families.

It is our prayer that this Regal book will help you discover biblical truth for your own life and help you meet the needs of others. May God richly bless you.

For a free catalog of resources from Regal Books/Gospel Light, please call your Christian supplier or contact us at 1-800-4-GOSPEL or www.regalbooks.com.

Library of Congress Cataloging-in-Publication Data
Laurie, Greg.
   Lies we tell ourselves / Greg Laurie.
      p. cm.
   ISBN 0-8307-4275-1 (trade paper)
   1. Truthfulness and falsehood—Religious aspects—Christianity.
   2. Common fallacies. 3. Temptation.   I. Title.
BV4627.F3L38 2006
241—dc22   2006024239

1   2   3   4   5   6   7   8   9   10   /   10   09   08   07   06

Rights for publishing this book in other languages are contracted by Gospel Light Worldwide, the international nonprofit ministry of Gospel Light. Gospel Light Worldwide also provides publishing and technical assistance to international publishers dedicated to producing Sunday School and Vacation Bible School curricula and books in the languages of the world. For additional information, visit www.gospellightworldwide.org, write to Gospel Light Worldwide, P.O. Box 3875, Ventura, CA 93006; or send an e-mail to info@gospellightworldwide.org.

CONTENTS

*Whenever trouble comes your way, let it be an opportunity
for joy. For when your faith is tested, your endurance has
a chance to grow. So let it grow, for when your endurance
is fully developed, you will be strong in character and ready
for anything. God blesses the people who patiently endure
testing. Afterward they will receive the crown of life
that God has promised to those who love him.*

JAMES 1:2-4,12, *NLT*

*I feel about airplanes the way I feel about diets. It seems to me
that they are wonderful things for other people to go on.*

JEAN KERR

I'M GOING ON A DIET TOMORROW

You never intended to become overweight.

The problem seemed to overtake you in the night, like fog stealing into San Francisco Bay. You woke up one morning, looked at yourself in the mirror and suddenly it dawned on you—*I have a weight problem! I'm overweight! I can't believe it.*

Denial, however, will only take you so far. Buying a new and more accurate bathroom scale probably won't tell you the story you want to hear. Difficult as it may be to admit, the evidence has been . . . well . . . expanding for some time.

Your pants are fitting tighter.

You find yourself tiring more easily.

You take a shower and nothing below your waist gets wet.

You get your shoes shined, and you have to take their word for it.

The couch gets up when you do.

Kids run to you to stay in the shade.

You find yourself developing a dependence on the color black as a fashion staple.

But there comes a point when even black can't cover reality. You have become a fat person—or at least you're well on your way. You might rationalize it by saying, "Well, there's just more of me to love now." But you really aren't fooling yourself or anyone else. Lying to yourself only covers the truth for a little while. Eventually, reality emerges.

You hate the idea of being fat, and you know you have to do something. So you actually start reading those e-mails about pills and amazing diets that will help you lose weight in 10 days or less. Those before-and-after pictures suddenly capture your attention.

Yet somehow . . . it all seems so unattainable.

Before I say any more, please understand that this isn't really a book about diets. It's more of a book about the lies we tell ourselves and how they get us into trouble in all sorts of areas in our lives. Becoming overweight? Well, that may not be an issue for you. But maybe telling little white lies is what you struggle with. Or maybe you wrestle with something more serious—

such as abusing drugs or alcohol, viewing pornography, or cheating on your spouse.

The good news is that before you reach the final page of this book, you'll be able to get a hold of a few timeless principles that will help you face down the rationalizations and excuses that have plagued you for years. You'll learn how to resist temptation of any sort—whether it pertains to calories or not.

Let's face it: We all need a better handle on this whole matter of talking ourselves into destructive and self-defeating behavior. So why all the emphasis on food and diets? The topic of diets provides an effective picture of how I've had to confront my own lame excuses . . . and what I've learned about facing temptation, 'fessing up to procrastination, and discovering the power to start on a new track. I hope that what I've learned will help you with whatever temptations you're facing.

THE BATTLE OF THE BULGE

For some reason, it seems as though my pants size has increased with the passing of years. For the longest time, I had a 32" waist and weighed 155 pounds. Not bad for someone 5' 11" (and a half). I felt good. I looked good. And amazingly, I held on to that number despite many late-night meals and a developing pattern of bad choices. One of my favorite indulgences came from a taco joint I frequented: a wicked thing called a Macho Combo Burrito. Just about every night at around 10 o'clock, I would pound down one of those "mother of all burritos."

Today, of course, the nightly ritual of slamming down a Macho Combo wouldn't even be an option for at least two reasons. Number one, I'd be wearing my burrito the next day. Number two, my stomach would be taking revenge on me all night long.

By the time I was tilting the bathroom scales at 188 pounds, I had to face the cold, hard truth that my metabolism was no longer what it used to be. I wasn't proud of my weight. Yet I couldn't deny it, because it had been memorialized at Nordstrom, of all places!

At the Nordstrom department store near our home, parents had been invited to add their children's names and ages on tiles to be permanently displayed on the floor of the children's department. A so-called friend of mine decided it would be cute to put my name and weight on one of those tiles for future generations to see. Right there at Nordstrom—next to "Amber, age 9" and "Nathan, age 6" is my tile. It proudly proclaims "Greg Laurie, 188." While a few people might wonder if I'm just a lot older than I look, most have probably guessed the sad truth.

EXTREME MEASURES

Once my weight had been immortalized for all to see while doing their back-to-school shopping for their kids, I decided that I needed to take a radical step. It was time to go on a diet.

Since then, I've been on about every kind of fad diet you've ever seen on a magazine cover. I think that I've actually tried them all. Sugar Busters? Been there, done that. Atkins? Makin' bacon! The Zone? Tried that one, too. The South Beach Diet? Okay, so I haven't tried that one, but it looks like another meat-and-cheese regimen to me—with a palm tree thrown in for effect.

Don't get me wrong—I believe that diets work. In fact, some work surprisingly well. The problem that most of us have is staying on a diet. The very word says it all: "diet," as in "die." In other words, deny yourself. Abstain.

We don't like the sound of words like that. Especially when we're out to dinner at a nice place and the waiter comes around with a dessert tray . . . and flan cake.

A while back, my wife, Cathe, and I were enjoying dinner with another couple at one of our favorite restaurants. After dining on some delicious and healthy grilled fish and vegetables, the server approached us with the inevitable dessert tray. Even the way restaurant employees approach the subject gives you a pretty good indication of where it will all lead.

"Can I tempt you with a dessert?" she asked.

"Tempt?" I replied.

"It's not a sin to be tempted, right?"

I listened to our server's memorized presentation. Servers often use words that should tip us off, such as "decadent" or "sinfully delicious." Then there's the "wicked devil's food cake."

It just so happened that this particular restaurant had my favorite dessert of all time. It's a savory little dish called flan cake. My wife could explain how they make it, but it's basically a moist cake in custard sauce with freshly whipped cream and strawberries. Then . . . just to finish it off . . . a little caramel sauce is artfully drizzled over the top. It makes my mouth water just to write about it!

I had already steeled myself for the approach of the dessert tray. So it really wasn't that difficult for me to say "no thank you" as the server went through the options.

Until she came to the flan cake.

Instantly, like a shark instinctively responding to the smell of blood, I was already imagining the flan cake in front of me. "Yeah, let's order that," I said, feeling the eyes of everyone at the table, "because I'm going on a diet tomorrow!"

At that, everyone at the table broke out laughing. When I asked why, they reminded me that I said the same thing every time this particular dessert was offered. It dawned on me that I had been rationalizing my flan cake indulgence for a long time. I'd been telling myself a lie every time I wanted to enjoy my favorite dessert.

That moment served as the inspiration for this book. It even inspired the title: *Lies We Tell Ourselves.* You now hold in your hands the fulfillment of that little moment of truth that I had in front of the dessert tray.

THE DEVIL MADE ME DO IT!

Well, I've carried on about my immortalized weight, my attempts at dieting and my weakness for flan cake. But again, this really isn't a book about obesity, desserts or diets. Instead, it's about the temptations that come our way and the ways we confront them, stare them down and overcome them. Sooner or later, temptation will come your way. You play a key role in how effectively you resist it.

A number of years ago, comedian Flip Wilson played Geraldine, a character who often shouted, "The devil made me do it!" While that line was good for a laugh, and while it is true that Satan plays a role in tempting us, the fact is that we must cooperate with the devil in order to give in to the temptation. In fact, temptation is Satan's primary method of attack. Interestingly, while we don't enjoy being tempted, we all know a lot about it and about giving in to it. Temptation is something that every Christian experiences.

The good news is that we can resist temptation. Jesus promises to help.

The apostle James wrote, "Blessed is the man who endures temptation" (Jas. 1:12). A better translation of the word "blessed" would be "happy." Happy is the person who resists temptation!

That's the main message of this book. Giving in to temptation won't really make you happy. Resisting it will. So let's dig deeper into how we can resist those times when temptation dangles in front of our face like an irresistible carrot placed in front of a horse.

FOR REFLECTION

Before you move on to chapter 1, I want to encourage you to apply what you've read so far to your own life. Ponder the following questions and be honest with yourself as you try to answer. Spend some time in reflective thought and prayer, asking God to point out areas in which you need to rely on Him to help you with the temptations you face.

1. In case you overlooked the quote at the beginning of the introduction, let me repeat it here. Jean Kerr wrote, "I feel about airplanes the way I feel about diets. It seems to me that they are wonderful things for other people to go on." Do you ever find yourself thinking this same way about sin?

2. Do you sometimes have the attitude that Scripture's guidelines apply to everyone else, but it's okay for you to break the rules?

3. What about areas of life that may seem less important—such as sneaking ahead in line at the grocery store or a movie?

4. How would you rewrite Jean Kerr's quote to reflect the area in your life in which this attitude is most pervasive?

5. How would you rewrite the quote to reflect the right attitude God wants you to have about temptation and sin?

6. I briefly shared my struggle with weight gain and poor food choices. Did you see

yourself as I described my own struggles with temptations related to food?

7. If not, what temptations do you struggle with?

8. What's your favorite excuse or rationalization for continuing a behavior that you know doesn't match up to your faith?

Spend some time in prayer asking God to help you see areas of life in which you lie to yourself or rationalize your behavior. Ask Him to help you surrender those areas of life to Him and depend on Him for strength to resist.

Remember, no one who wants to do wrong should ever say, "God is tempting me." God is never tempted to do wrong, and he never tempts anyone else either. Temptation comes from the lure of our own evil desires.

JAMES 1:13-14, *NLT*

Trials, temptations, disappointments—all these are helps instead of hindrances, if one uses them rightly. They not only test the fiber of character but strengthen it. Every conquering temptation represents a new fund of moral energy. Every trial endured and weathered in the right spirit makes a soul nobler and stronger than it was before.

JAMES BUCKHAM

THE TRUTH ABOUT TEMPTATION

During a busy lunch hour in a crowded downtown, a pastor frantically searched for a parking place. He circled several blocks again and again, but a car sat at every meter and every parking ramp flashed a "Full" sign. Desperate to get to an important meeting, the pastor finally decided to double-park. He took out his business card and wrote a note in case a police officer might come by to ticket him.

"Dear Officer," the pastor wrote, "I circled this block a dozen times, but I could not find a place to park. I have an appointment to keep." Smiling to himself, he closed his note with, "Forgive us our trespasses."

About an hour later, the pastor returned to find a parking ticket under his windshield wiper. Handwritten on the back of the ticket were these words: "Dear Reverend, I have patrolled this block for a dozen years.

If I don't give you a ticket, I'll lose my job." The officer had signed his name and badge number, and then added the kicker: "Lead us not into temptation."

"Lead us not into temptation!" Those words are from what we call the Lord's Prayer, one of the most well-known passages in the Bible. This reminds me of a bumper sticker I once read: *"Lead us not into temptation. We can easily find it ourselves!"*

We generally think that all temptation is bad. Yet it may surprise you to know that testing, and even temptation, can have a positive effect. The Bible tells us, "Blessed is the man who endures temptation; for when he has been approved, he will receive the crown of life which the Lord has promised to those who love Him" (Jas. 1:12).

Right off the bat, from this verse we learn three things about temptation:

1. We can endure temptation: "Blessed is the man [or woman] who endures temptation."

2. God promises a reward when we endure it: "He [or she] will receive the crown of life."

3. We will be happier people if we resist the pull of temptation: "Blessed is the man [or woman] who endures."

Martin Luther once said, "One Christian who has been tempted is worth a thousand who haven't." It's also been said, "Christians are a lot like tea bags. You don't know what they're made of until you put them in hot water."

You never know when temptation will come your way. I once heard about a young salesman who went to bid on a job for his firm. When he was ushered into the purchasing agent's office, he couldn't help but notice a competitor's bid lying there on the desk. Unfortunately, the actual figure was covered by a can of juice. The temptation to see the amount soon became too much for the salesman, and he slowly lifted the can. As he did so, thousands of BBs poured from the bottomless container and scattered across the floor. His heart sank. It was a trap, and he got busted for giving in to his temptation.

And you and I will, too. That's why we must learn to resist temptation. Benjamin Franklin once wrote, "It is easier to suppress the first desire than to satisfy all that follow it."

WHAT YOU NEED TO KNOW ABOUT TEMPTATION

In the next few pages, we'll be getting up close and personal with this whole issue of temptation. In fact, we'll zero in on some very specific questions, such as:

- When does temptation come?
- Where does it come from?
- Whom does it come to?

In Luke 4, we find the story of Jesus being tempted by Satan. We'll look at this account again later in more detail. While this story recorded in Scripture is brief—hardly more than a few verses—it is filled with truths that can help us face the daily barrage of temptations that come our way at breakneck speed. Jesus set the example.

Now, let's set the scene. Jesus was ready to officially begin His public ministry. But before that could happen, He had to take a couple of very important steps. The first was to be baptized. The other was to face His temptation in the wilderness.

Have you ever wondered why Jesus needed to be baptized? He had never sinned! He had no need to undergo the baptism of repentance that his cousin, John the Baptizer, was advocating. So why did Jesus do it? Because He wanted to set an example for all of us. And that, by the way, is also why He faced this series of temptations.

It's essential that we see Jesus as a man facing Satan. In other words, Jesus did not use His divine power to be delivered or to run Satan out. He showed us how to handle temptation when it comes our way. Jesus occupied ground that we can occupy as we heed the words of Philippians 2:5: "Let this mind be in you which was also in Christ Jesus."

As Christians, we constantly face at least three enemies—the flesh, the world and the devil. The *flesh* is the evil desire we all have within us—that vulnerability or propensity to do the wrong thing. The *world* is the place where we can find all kinds of temptations that lure us into indulging in our evil desires. The *devil,* of course, is Satan, who wants us to give in to our evil desires because that will—at least temporarily—build walls in our relationship with God.

Another way to think about these three enemies is to consider the flesh, with its evil desires, as the internal foe. The world, with its enticements, is the external foe. And Satan, with his temptations, is the infernal foe.

It can seem so tough to resist temptation. After all, temptation is so . . . *tempting!* Yet the effect of giving in to temptation can be absolutely devastating. By yielding to temptation, in just a split second we can lose everything that it might have taken an entire lifetime for us to gain. However, in order to be able to resist temptation, it's important for us to first understand where temptation comes from, when it attacks, what its target is and how it gains a toehold in our life. This brings us to the first question I raised.

WHEN DOES TEMPTATION COME?

The simple answer is that while temptation can come at any time, it often comes after we experience times of great blessing.

Jesus' encounter with the evil one took place almost immediately after His baptism and the public affirmation by His Father—what must have been one of the great highlights of His earthly life. When Jesus came up out of the muddy waters of the Jordan, something incredible happened. The Bible says that heaven was opened and the Holy Spirit descended upon Jesus in the form of a dove. Then the Father spoke from heaven: "This is My beloved Son, in whom I am well pleased" (Matt. 3:17).

That's when Satan bared his teeth: "Then Jesus, being filled with the Holy Spirit, returned from the Jordan and was led by the Spirit into the wilderness, being tempted for forty days by the devil" (Luke 4:1-2). Just as Satan followed the dove, trial and temptation often come after great blessing. Strange as it might seem, the two often go hand in hand.

Think about this for a minute. When we face temptation as Christians, we almost instinctively wonder what we're doing wrong. Or we wonder if God is some-how punishing us. We might even try to willfully change some part of our life in which we think we're disap-pointing God or failing Him.

While it's great to try to live without sin in our lives, the truth is that temptation generally comes after times when we've experienced great blessings from God. So, you might be in church some Sunday, being encouraged in your faith, and right after the service—perhaps even during—some shockingly impure thought or some ungodly impulse tugs on you. *Good night*, you wonder, *where did* that *come from?* However, as a matter of fact, we should expect to face temptation whenever we have experienced great blessing.

History tells us that when Hitler invaded Euro-pean nations during the early years of World War II, in almost every situation, he attacked on a weekend. You see, Hitler knew that the various national governments would not be in session, which would make it more dif-ficult for them to react swiftly to an invasion.

In much the same way, the devil—the enemy of our souls—watches and waits for an opportune time to launch his invasion. He bides his time, looking for that moment when we are most vulnerable. Strange as it might seem, that vulnerable moment can take place when we imagine ourselves to be at our strongest.

The apostle Paul had a succinct word of warning along those lines: "Therefore let him who thinks he stands take heed lest he fall" (1 Cor. 10:12).

WHERE DOES TEMPTATION COME FROM?

Have you ever fallen into sin and—somewhat amazed that you gave in to the temptation—asked yourself how you got there? You probably went through a series of events that ultimately led you to rationalize your sin. We'll look more at rationalization and excuses in the next chapter, but for now let's examine the series of events that led to the sin.

Temptation often enters in through the realm of your imagination. Picture it as an unwelcome visitor knocking at your door. You know that if you open the door, you'll have trouble. So when the enemy comes with temptation, don't open the door. In fact, don't even look through the peephole! Don't underestimate sin or the power of it.

In addition, keep in mind that we play a vital role in resisting or giving in to our own temptation. It's true. Interestingly, when we resist temptation, we are pretty quick to take credit for our strong faith. But when we give in to temptation, it's easy to blame God for allowing us to fail. James wrote:

Let no one say when he is tempted, "I am tempted by God"; for God cannot be tempted by evil,
nor does He Himself tempt anyone. But each
one is tempted when he is drawn away by his
own desires and enticed. Then, when desire has
conceived, it gives birth to sin; and sin, when it
is full-grown, brings forth death. Do not be
deceived, my beloved brethren (Jas. 1:13–16).

The truth is, sin is an inside job. Temptation itself
starts with our bent toward doing the wrong thing.
Where there's no desire on our part, there's no real
temptation. Satan needs our cooperation to give in to
his temptation. Think about it: Have you ever seen an
insurance salesman walking up and down among the
grave markers in a cemetery, trying to make a sale?
I don't think so. That's because you can't sell something
to someone who isn't listening to you and doesn't care
about what you have to say.

The same is true of us. The devil needs our willing
assistance. He's going door to door looking for a cus-
tomer who'll invite him in.

But when we get down to it, we have only ourselves
to thank when we give in to temptation. Jesus said,
"What comes out of a man, that defiles a man" (Mark
7:20). Paul echoed this thought when he wrote, "Don't

you realize that whatever you choose to obey becomes your master? You can choose sin, which leads to death, or you can choose to obey God and receive his approval" (Rom. 6:16, *NLT*).

The Scorpion and the Tortoise

Yes, we have our own sinful nature to blame for most of our problems. This reminds me of the fable of the scorpion and the tortoise. As you may or may not know, scorpions can't really swim. So, one day, a scorpion that wanted to cross a pond found a rather unsuspecting tortoise and asked if he would give him a lift to the other side.

"Are you joking?" the tortoise exclaimed. "You'll sting me while I'm swimming, and I'll drown."

"My dear tortoise," laughed the scorpion, "if I were to sting you, you would drown, and I'd go down with you. Now, where is the logic in that?"

"You've got a point there," reasoned the tortoise. "Hop on."

The scorpion climbed aboard. Halfway across the pond, he carefully aimed his powerful stinger and gave the tortoise everything he had.

As they both began to sink, the tortoise, resigned to his fate, turned to the scorpion and said, "Do you mind if I ask you something? You said there was no logic in your stinging me. Why did you do it?"

"It has nothing to do with logic," the drowning scorpion replied. "It's just my nature!"

That's not a bad description of temptation—and why we're so weak. In the immortal words of the scorpion, "It's just our nature." We all have a natural, inward bent to do the wrong thing. We like to think that our bad behavior is a direct result of our upbringing, environment, and so on. Although those things do have an influence on us, the primary reason we think and do the wrong things is because of the sinful nature within each one of us.

"I Couldn't Resist Myself"

When my son Jonathan was still very young, I sent him to bed one night with some clear instructions: "Now, turn off the light. No more video games, okay?"

He agreed. But a bit later, I noticed a familiar, blue glow coming from beneath the door to his room. When I opened the door, I caught little Jonathan red-handed, blasting away at enemy spaceships. When I demanded an explanation, he blurted out, "Dad, I didn't mean to, but I couldn't resist myself."

His response was so cute that I just let it go (after unplugging the video game, of course). But my little boy was really on to something. We love to blame the devil and others for our spiritual stumbles and falls. But the truth is, it's just our nature. Or, as that young theologian Jonathan Laurie put it, "I couldn't resist myself."

When we give in to our temptation, we like to rationalize and conveniently place the blame on someone or something else. (It was that waitress's fault for waving that dessert tray with flan cake beneath my nose!) Sometimes, we even want to blame God for our missteps. We will lamely say something along the lines of, "God just gave me more than I could handle!" Talk about passing the buck! This is what Adam essentially did in the Garden, and it's what we do when we can't own up to our own complicity in our sinful choices.

The Bible clearly refutes this kind of thinking, reminding us, "Let no one say when he is tempted, 'I am tempted by God'; for God cannot be tempted by evil, nor does He Himself tempt anyone" (Jas. 1:13). Scripture also tells us that God will never give us more than we can handle: "No temptation has seized you except what is common to man. And God is faithful; he will not let you be tempted beyond what you can bear. But when you are tempted, he will also provide a way out so that you can stand up under it" (1 Cor. 10:13, *NIV*).

WHOM DOES TEMPTATION COME TO?

In a broad sense, everyone is tempted. At the same time, without question, the enemy focuses his attacks on those who are young in the faith and those who are making a difference—or potentially could make a difference—for the kingdom of God.

I think practically every new Christian doubts his or her salvation in some way. It might be the day after you ask Jesus to come into your life, and the devil whispers in your ear, "Do you actually believe that God would forgive someone like you? Do you really think your sins are forgiven and Jesus lives in your heart? Get real! You psyched yourself into it!" You may not sense God's nearness at that particular moment, and as a result, you start believing that Satan's lies are the truth.

Maybe you recall being hit with some serious temptations when you first came to know Jesus as your Savior. The same kind of temptation will also come whenever you tell God, "I want You to use me." Please know that this is common, and even to be expected to a large degree, among those who are new in the faith or who invite God to use them. You need to realize that Satan will attack. So be aware.

In the Parable of the Sower, Jesus gives us some insight into how Satan works. He compares God's

Word to seed being sown by a farmer. Some of the seed falls on the road, and the ever-watching birds quickly swoop down and scoop it up. Jesus then goes on to interpret these words: "And these are the ones by the wayside where the word is sown. When they hear, Satan comes immediately and takes away the word that was sown in their hearts" (Mark 4:15).

Notice the words, "Satan comes immediately." In other words, the enemy likes to attack before a young believer can be established in the faith or before he or she has the opportunity to send down roots into the nourishing soil of God's Word. I myself remember experiencing a major temptation in my life right after my conversion.

A Pretty Girl Comes Calling

When I asked Jesus to be my Lord and Savior, I was in high school. I was just days old in the faith and bubbling over with excitement about what God had done for me. I even wore a little button on my shirt with a drawing of Jesus on it.

I went to one of my classes, where I noticed an attractive girl looking at me and smiling. Now, I had noticed this girl before, but frankly, she had never noticed me. Suddenly—seemingly out of nowhere—she was making eyes at me!

The Christians I knew had told me that I probably would face temptations after my conversion. I remember wondering in that moment, *Could this be it?* I didn't have to wait long to find out, because just as class let out, this cute little dish sashayed up to me and said, "Hi. What's your name?"

I forgot my name momentarily, stunned by her sudden interest in me.

"You're really cute, Greg," she cooed. "I've never noticed you before."

I was dumbfounded. Then she looked into my eyes and said, "I would really like to get to know you better. Hey, my parents have this house up in the mountains, and they'll be gone this weekend. Want to go up with me?"

I knew this had to be a temptation. Things like this just didn't happen to me! I wondered, *Why is this happening to me now, when I can't act on it? Talk about bad timing!* Then it dawned on me: This wasn't bad timing. It was precise timing—from hell. Satan was hitting me where I was weak and when I was young in the faith.

I got excited, not so much about the temptation, but about the opportunity to resist. I remember thinking that if Satan wanted to trip me up that much, God must have something really special in store for me. So, by the grace of God, I said no to her. She walked off in a huff, and I'm sure she quickly found another taker for her little mountain getaway.

As a new follower of Jesus Christ, I felt a great sense of relief and joy as I made my first conscious decision to turn away from what I wanted to do. And I was blessed— or happy—as the Scripture says we will be when we resist temptation (see Jas. 1:12).

God knows exactly how much we can take. When He lets His children go through fiery trials, He always keeps one eye on them and one finger on the thermostat. Remember, He has made a way of escape in the midst of every temptation. Thus, if we succumb to the enticements and temptations of the devil, we must take responsibility for our actions.

Temptation Knocks at Every Door
Why did Satan tempt all kinds of people throughout Scripture? In nearly every case, it is because of the damage they were doing to his evil kingdom. Again, be forewarned. When you pray, "Lord, let my life make a difference," you'd better brace yourself. The enemy won't sit idly by.

This is why Satan attacked Jesus. Jesus was a threat to him. And this is why he will attack you, because you, as God's follower, also represent a threat to him. You might protest and say, "But, Greg, I never get tempted to do the wrong thing!" If that's the case, then you must be either dead or worthless. As the great British preacher C. H. Spurgeon once wrote, "You don't kick a dead horse."

If you are really following Jesus, you will be tempted. It's not a matter of if—it's a matter of when and how.

FOR REFLECTION

Before you move on to chapter 2, I want to encourage you to apply what you've read here to your own life. Ponder the following questions and be honest with yourself as you try to answer. I suggest that you spend time in reflective thought and prayer, asking God to point out areas in which you need to rely on Him to help you with the temptations you face.

1. When you face temptation, who do you blame? Do you blame God or Satan or yourself? Why?

2. In your own experience, have you faced temptation during times of great blessing?

3. Have you faced temptation during times when you have asked God to use you to make a difference in His kingdom?

4. Why do you think the enemy steps up his attacks against new believers and those who are trying to serve God completely?

5. In this chapter, I described a temptation that I faced when I first became a follower of Jesus and how I realized that I was being tempted. Can you think of a similar situation in which you realized you were facing a temptation right in the middle of the experience?

6. How did you resist the temptation?

7. What have you learned from your own experience of resisting temptation that might be helpful for repelling future attacks?

This command I am giving you today is not too difficult for you to understand or perform. It is not up in heaven, so distant that you must ask, "Who will go to heaven and bring it down so we can hear and obey it?" It is not beyond the sea, so far away that you must ask, "Who will cross the sea to bring it to us so we can hear and obey it?" The message is very close at hand; it is on your lips and in your heart so that you can obey it.

DEUTERONOMY 30:11-14, *NLT*

'Tis one thing to be tempted, another thing to fall.

WILLIAM SHAKESPEARE

EXCUSES, EXCUSES

What's your favorite excuse? I have a whole list of excuses whenever I'm faced with straightening up my office. I don't like to admit it, but I will allow my office to decline to a rather sorry state before I plunge in and clean things up.

Before that happens, however, it can get pretty bad. I stack books on top of books and pile layers of paper on top of older layers of paper (in geology, this is known as a sedimentary formation). My morning latte from two days ago, cold and half consumed, balances forlornly on the last available flat surface.

I will put off cleaning up after myself as long as possible. I am the classic procrastinator. I operate by that old adage, "Don't do today what you can put off until tomorrow." Finally, I get sick of living in the mess and the need to conduct a major excavation project to find anything. So I fly into action. Like a whirlwind or the Tazmanian Devil of Warner Brothers fame, I sweep through to purge my desk of garbage piles and bring books and paperwork back to a place of order.

I'm guessing that I'm not the only excuse-maker around. I have a hunch that you might fall into those tendencies, too. Otherwise, why would you have picked up this book or read this far? Take heart. There are plenty more of us out there.

An article in *USA Today* dealt with the penchant that nearly all of us have for making excuses. It pointed out that each of us fibs at least 50 times per day! According to the article, "We lie about our age, our income, or our accomplishments. And we use lies to escape embarrassment."[1]

The most commonly used excuses? See if these don't sound strangely familiar:

"I wasn't feeling well."

"I didn't want to hurt your feelings."

"I was only trying to help."

"I was just kidding."

And then there's that all-time classic: "The check is in the mail."[2]

LAME EXCUSES

I found a website that lists actual excuses people have used to get out of showing up for work. Apparently, their employers found the alibis so outrageous that they thought the responses should be saved for posterity—or at least shared with others as a form of entertainment. Here are just a few of them:

"I won't be in today. My fish is sick, and I need to take it to the vet."

"I won't be in today because I have come down with spring fever."

"I can't come to work today because the city is paving my street, and I can't get out!"

"I will not be in to work today because my parents' dog died."

Left on an employer's answering machine: "Sorry, boss, I won't be in for three days. Went to see my sister off on her cruise to the Bahamas . . . darn ship left with me still on it. The captain refuses to turn back."

At least one guy who called in was honest about it. He said to his boss, "I am sick with the 'lack'—the lack of ambition."[3]

Then there are those doozies of excuses that people lay on police officers when they've been nailed for speeding. One obviously inebriated man was pulled over by the California Highway Patrol because he was driving the wrong way on the freeway. To say the least, this was not a particularly healthy activity. The officer who pulled over the man could hardly contain himself as he shouted, "Sir, do you know you were driving down the interstate the wrong way?"

The drunk responded, "How do you know? You don't know where I live!"

Ah, the logic of an alcohol-soaked brain. Needless to say, this man spent the night in jail.

Another man stopped for speeding actually said to the officer, "Please excuse me from this speeding ticket. You see, my wife ran off with a state policeman, and when I saw your flashing lights, I didn't stop because I thought you might be the trooper who was trying to bring her back to me!" I don't know if he was given a ticket for speeding or not, but he should have been arrested for giving a lame excuse.

As George Washington said, "It is better to offer no excuse than a bad one."

THE DEFINITION OF AN EXCUSE

When it comes to temptation, we all know what it's like to justify something we're about to do with a clever excuse. You know the routine.

"I know this is wrong, but everybody's doing it."

"I'll know when to stop."

"I'll quit tomorrow."

"It's not my fault."

"I can't help it—I've been under so much stress."

"I'm really not hurting anyone but myself."

"I deserve this."

"I'm not that bad."

"It's totally acceptable in other cultures."

"God understands my unique needs."

Do any of these sound familiar? As someone once said, "An excuse is nothing more than the skin of a reason stuffed with a lie." I think I'll be even bolder and declare that an excuse is a downright lie.

We usually offer such lies when we don't want to do something that we know we really ought to do—or when we do want to do something that we really ought not to do. Is there anyone who actually looks forward to mowing the lawn or taking out the trash or putting gas in the car? I don't know why, but I will put off filling up my car with gas as long as possible. Maybe it's because I think I'll somehow save money by waiting. I finally break down when that little light (sometimes called an "idiot light"—and for good reason) comes on. Reluctantly, I will pull into the nearest gas station and do that which I dreaded. And I find it really isn't that bad.

The fact is, we've all heard and used excuses at one time or another, and most of the time, they're not all that creative. Worse, we're lying to ourselves and to anyone we give our excuses to. Since humanity's beginning in the Garden of Eden, we have made poor excuses.

THE FIRST EXCUSE

The first recorded excuse was made by the first man himself, Adam. Talk about a guy who had it made in the shade. He was created by God and placed in a paradise so lush and lovely it would make Maui look like a parking lot. Surrounded by intense, unimaginable beauty and splendor, Adam had a life we can barely imagine. Think about it—there was no pollution, no discomfort, no aging and, best of all, no death.

Even more, Adam's basic job description required him to discover, enjoy and watch over all that God had made. Best of all, the Lord Himself showed up each and every day, and He and Adam talked over the events of the day. This took place just as the sun was setting, before nightfall.

So there was Adam, living large and enjoying fellowship with God Himself. Each day, he would be greeted by a new discovery of what his Friend and Creator had made. Yet something was missing in Adam's life. Sure, he liked to hang out with animals, admire the scenery and visit with his Creator every day. But something in him wanted someone else with whom he could share all these things. And that someone didn't yet exist.

You know how the story goes. One day, the Lord had Adam fall into a deep sleep. When Adam awoke, there, for the first time, was that someone he'd been longing for. He called her Eve. She was beautiful to behold, and she became Adam's close friend, second only to God Himself.

You couldn't ask for a better life.

However, God had given Adam and his new bride a dangerous ability—the power to choose. They could choose to do right and follow their Creator. Or they could choose to turn their back on Him and go their own way.

"But why?" we ask. "Why didn't God just make Adam want to do the right thing? Why did He give him the opportunity to choose, with all the potential for danger that those choices involved?" The answer to that question really is not very complicated. God wanted voluntary love, not forced affection. Would you want someone to be your friend because he or she had to be, or because that person truly wanted to have a relationship with you? And so it was with the Creator.

THE CHOICE

So God gave to His two finest creations the ability to choose, and you probably know what they did—the Bible tells the whole sad story in Genesis 3. Adam and

Eve deliberately disobeyed God and ate of the forbidden fruit. Now, considering the fact that Adam and Eve lived in a perfect paradise, there had to be something very attractive about this fruit that caught their eye. Who knows? Maybe it glowed in the dark or pulsated.

What we do know is that this fruit just flat out looked good. Really good. It probably smelled pretty amazing, too. (For some reason, whenever I imagine the fruit in the Garden that tempted Adam and Eve, I think about big, juicy, ripe peaches, hanging on the limb in the golden pink light of a new day. Now, that would tempt me!) So, despite the fact that their Creator and Best Friend had warned them and told them not to do it, Adam and Eve each were tempted to the point that they finally gave in and took a bite. They even might have made an excuse and said, "It's really all right, because we won't ever do it again!"

But they wouldn't have to. Once was enough.

More than enough.

We are still living with the consequences of their little taste test to this very day: war, terrorism, aging, disease, divorce, death and, worst of all, separation from God Himself. It all came from that first turning away from God in a place that had been—but could be no longer—a paradise.

GOD ALWAYS KEEPS HIS APPOINTMENTS

The story goes on. Right on schedule, just like every other day, God showed up for His regular appointment with Adam.

While it occurred at the same time and in the same place, nothing could ever be the same again. For the first time ever, Adam didn't show. Genesis tells us, "They heard the sound of the LORD God walking in the garden in the cool of the day" (3:8).

The Creator called out, "Adam, where are you?" (see v. 9). God didn't say this because He couldn't figure out which bush His two children were hiding behind. They hadn't stumped Him any more than a father playing Hide and Seek with his two-year-old. God called out for a reason. He wanted His friend to come clean and to admit what he had done.

In days past, Adam must have looked forward to his meeting with God each and every day. I know I would have. When something would come up, Adam might have thought, *I must talk to the Lord about that in our time together later this afternoon.* Or perhaps after making a new discovery in the Garden that he was commanded to tend, he would decide to ask God about it: "Lord, how did You ever come up with this design?"

It's interesting to note that God didn't come in the heat of the day, so Adam would think God was approaching him in the heat of His anger. And God didn't come in the early morning, so that Adam would think that God was waiting to nail him for his sin. After all, the Bible teaches, "The LORD is merciful and gracious, slow to anger, and abounding in mercy" (Ps. 103:8).

Instead, the Lord came in the cool of the day, as Adam's loving, patient, grieved yet understanding Creator and Friend. At the same time, however, God had to confront this thing that had invaded His perfect world. And He expected an accounting from Adam.

Now, instead of looking forward with joy to this daily event as Adam usually did, he shrank from it. Instead of the appointment filling him with anticipation and joy, it overwhelmed him with dread.

Sin will do that to you. It will quench your appetite for what you really need, while increasing your hunger for what can ultimately destroy you. God had given Adam plenty of time to think about what he had done. What for a fleeting moment had seemed so exciting and intoxicating was now having its ultimate effect. A dead, empty feeling had settled over Adam and Eve.

Sin was doing its corrosive work in the first couple. They were experiencing something they had never known before. We know that feeling. It's called guilt.

And it was terrible. It gnawed at Adam's insides, giving him no rest. He must have kept repeating to himself, *If only I hadn't taken that bite!* As Adam sat there, his mind filled with these unfamiliar tormenting thoughts, he suddenly heard a familiar voice.

"Adam?"

Oh, no! Panic flooded Adam, turning his insides to ice water. It was the Lord! *What am I gonna say?* he must have thought. *How can I possibly explain this? How can I face Him?*

Adam grabbed Eve, and they quickly ducked for cover. They ran. They crouched. They hid.

"Adam, where are you?"

By the way, notice that instead of man calling out to God, it was God calling out to man. This is one significant thing that distinguishes the Christian faith from any other belief system or religion in the world. In all religions apart from Christianity, for all practical purposes, man must repeatedly call out to God.

But the Bible describes a very different reality. From the very beginning of Scripture, God called out to man. And He still does. He's still calling. Just as He called out to Adam in the Garden long ago, He calls out to us today.

A FASCINATING QUESTION

"Adam, where are you?" Why did God call out to His wayward son? Among other things, He wanted to convince

Adam of his sin. We need God to pursue us in these kinds of situations because we are so good at rationalizing our sin—in such a way that we don't even think we've done anything wrong.

Reminds me of an overweight person making excuses for eating his flan cake!

What tone of voice do you think God used that day in the Garden? Do you think it was harsh and loud? "Adam, where are you, you miserable failure?" I don't think so. Do you imagine that maybe the Lord felt a little bewildered and confused? "Adam, where in the world are you? I can't find you!" Not a chance.

I think Adam and Eve heard the voice of a grieved but loving Father.

So here was Adam, sneaking around, crouching in the brush, hiding behind his coverup. Satan had promised that if Adam and Eve ate of the forbidden fruit, they would be "like God, knowing good and evil" (Gen. 3:5). So God was essentially saying, "Well, Adam, is that how it is? Or did the devil lie to you?"

The same thing happens to us. Satan whispers in our ear, "Go for it! This will be fun! No one will ever know!" And the Lord speaks quietly in our heart, "Is that how it turned out? Are you pleased with the outcome?"

"Where are you?" When you think about it, God's call for Adam really was a fascinating question for the

Creator to ask. God, of course, knew exactly where Adam and Eve were. He wasn't calling them to get information, but rather a confession. He wanted them to confront what they'd done so that they could set things right and be restored to fellowship with Him. God wanted Adam and Eve to come out of the stupor of sin and admit their real condition.

But why was that necessary?

Did God want to rub Adam's nose in it? Hardly. The reason God called for Adam is the same reason the Holy Spirit will convict us—and even use guilt. God wants to awaken us, open our eyes and turn us around. God wants us to run to Him, not away from Him. But Adam wasn't ready for that yet.

Finally, Adam answered, "I heard Your voice in the garden, and I was afraid because I was naked; and I hid myself" (Gen. 3:10). God immediately responded, "Who told you that you were naked?" (v. 11).

Now, why did God ask such a question? Didn't He already know the answer to this one as well? Yes, but he wanted Adam to know, too. Have you ever known that your child had done something wrong and you confronted him or her? You might have asked your child, "Did you do such and such? Why did you do that? Do you think this is all right for you to do?" Did you ask your child these questions because you personally didn't know what was right or wrong? Of course not. You asked because you wanted to make sure your child knew it was wrong. You were looking for an admission of wrongdoing, a confession of sin. And that's exactly what God was looking for from Adam, too.

THE GREATEST EXCUSE ON EARTH

Adam then offered up the first recorded excuse ever given by man. And it was a whopper.

He not only failed to acknowledge personal responsibility, but he also quickly looked around for someone else to blame. And since there was only one other human being in the whole world besides himself, he blamed her. Adam told the Lord, "The woman whom You gave to be with me, she gave me of the tree, and I ate" (Gen. 3:12).

This shows the absolute wickedness of sin. The Scripture is clear that while Eve had been deceived, it was Adam who willfully and knowingly sinned. If that weren't bad enough, he had the audacity to actually blame God for it! In essence, Adam was saying, "You, Lord, have sinned! This is Your doing. It's the woman You gave me! I was doing just fine, and then You brought Eve along!"

How easily God could have struck down Adam where he stood. Like a spoiled little child, Adam dared to suggest that it was God, and not him, who had failed. God had literally put Adam in paradise with every possible comfort, surrounded by breathtaking beauty, and even provided him with a beautiful companion. Yet in spite of all this, Adam lashed out at the very God who had given all this to him. But as Lamentations reminds us, "The unfailing love of the LORD never ends! By his mercies we have been kept from complete destruction" (3:22, *NLT*).

Neither Adam nor Eve convinced God with their excuses. God busted His wayward children, and separation from Him resulted.

How did all of this happen in the first place?

It began with temptation. The First Couple considered temptation, entertained it and then gave in to it.

WHERE ARE YOU?

Has God been seeking you recently?

"I missed you in church this last week! Where are you?"

"I missed hearing from you in prayer today! Where are you?"

"You read your Bible this morning, but with such an absent mind. Where are you?"

Where are you spiritually in your life right now? Are you in the place you need to be? Are you satisfied with your spiritual condition, or does a change need to take place? Before you can find your way to what you need, you must first recognize where you are. And if you have courage to ask God that question, He'll tell you.

Let's say you wanted to come to our church for a Sunday morning service, so you give us a call. When I pick up the phone, you ask, "How do we get to Harvest Christian Fellowship? We want to worship with you this morning!"

You know, of course, what my next question will be: "Where are you?" Now, why would I ask that? Is it because I'm really nosy and want to know your every step? Not at all. The reason I'm asking where you are is so that I can tell you how to get to where you want to go.

So, why did God ask Adam, "Where are you?" God wanted to tell Adam how to get back to paradise.

Perhaps you're thinking, *In a spiritual sense, I don't know where I am at all. I only know that I'm not where I ought to be or where I want to be. That's all I can say.* But that's good. It's a beginning. That's where it all starts.

Admit that you have lost your way. God wants to tell you how to get back to the paradise of a right relationship with Him.

FOR REFLECTION

Before you move on to chapter 3, I want to encourage you to apply what you've read here to your own life. Ponder the following questions and be honest with yourself as you try to answer. I suggest that you spend some time in reflective thought and prayer, asking God to point out areas in your life in which you need to rely on Him to help you.

1. This chapter started with the question, "What's your favorite excuse?" Between you and God, answer that question as it relates to a temptation that you give in to over and over again.

2. What excuse do you regularly tell yourself? "I know this is wrong, but everybody's doing it"; "I'll know when to stop"; "I'll quit tomorrow"; "I can't help it, I've been under so much stress"; "I'm really not hurting anyone but myself"; or do you use some other excuse to rationalize your sinful choices?

3. In this chapter, I asked why God gave Adam the opportunity to choose when He knew

the potential for danger involved in those choices. I answered the question with the simple statement that God desired voluntary love, not forced affection. What do you think we'd be like if God didn't allow us to choose whether we obey or disobey Him? Or whether or not we love Him?

4. As I asked earlier in the chapter, would you want someone to be your friend because he or she had to be or because he or she truly wanted to have a relationship with you? Why do you think God created us to have choices like this?

5. When you sense God's presence, do you have the urge to run and hide from Him? Or are you more likely to enjoy chatting with the Lord in the cool of the day?

6. What causes you either to run from God or to thoroughly enjoy His presence?

Chapter 2

Stand fast therefore in the liberty by which Christ has made
us free, and do not be entangled again with a yoke of
bondage. For you, brethren, have been called to liberty; only
do not use liberty as an opportunity for the flesh,
but through love serve one another.

GALATIANS 5:1,13

It takes less time to do a thing right than it does
to explain why you did it wrong.

HENRY WADSWORTH LONGFELLOW

Notes

1. Jerald Jellison, *USA Today*, quoted in "Little White Lies," *Bible.org*. http://www.bible.org/illus.asp?topic_id=894 (accessed February 8, 2005).
2. Ibid.
3. "Work Excuses," *Captain Cynic*. http://www.captaincynic.com/thread.php3/thrdid=13010-ufrmid=18 (accessed February 8, 2005).

MISSTEPS AND SECOND CHANCES

I'm often asked, "Can I do this and still be a Christian?"

Can I go to these movies? Can I listen to this kind of music? Can I go to this kind of place? Can I have this kind of relationship? Can I indulge in this pursuit and still technically be a believer?

Temptation doesn't always come in an extra-large shipping container. Sometimes, temptation comes in a much smaller form—a tiny but attractive package that Satan leaves on our doorstep. He delivers the dilemma of whether or not we should open the package. It's almost as if we have learned not to release the temptation that comes in the boxcar of a train or the cargo container from a ship, so Satan says, "Here's a much smaller gift of pleasure for you. C'mon—it won't hurt to open such a small package—to give in to such a little temptation."

What harm will it cause?

The apostle Paul said, "All things are lawful for me, but not all things are helpful; all things are lawful for me, but not all things edify" (1 Cor. 10:23). Or, as another translation puts it, "All things are legitimate, but not all things are constructive to character and edifying to spiritual life" (*AMP*).

On more than one occasion, the Bible compares the Christian life to running a race. So, when facing temptation, you need to consider whether this little thing you are wondering about will slow you down in the race of life. Will that questionable relationship stop you from making progress? Will that negative habit impair your performance? The writer of Hebrews instructs, "lay aside every weight, and the sin which so easily ensnares us, and let us run with endurance the race that is set before us" (Heb. 12:1).

If you're preparing to run a race, you don't carry a set of scuba tanks on your back in case you need oxygen, as that weight will slow you down. To run in a race, you must learn how to travel light. In the same way, if you want to run in the race of life, you must run light. So how do you determine what things are slowing you down?

WALKING A FINE LINE

If you have ever been lured by a small temptation and wondered whether it was allowable for you as a Christian, ask yourself these four questions:

1. **Does it build me up spiritually?** Giving in to a temptation in your life can tear you down if it rips you away from the people of God or dulls your hunger for the Word of God. If you like junk food and eat a lot of it, you won't have an appetite when it's time for a real meal. In the same way, you shouldn't take things in that will spoil your spiritual appetite.

2. **Does it bring me under its power?** Paul wrote, "All things are lawful for me, but I will not be brought under the power of any" (1 Cor. 6:12). When you face one of these seemingly small temptations, decide if you want to be under the power of anyone or anything but Jesus Christ. Personally, I don't want to be under the power of drugs. I don't want to be under the power of alcohol. I don't want to be under the power of tobacco. If you find yourself giving in to a small temptation and it then gets a hold on you, you need to cut it loose.

3. **Do I have an uneasy conscience about it?** To the Christians in Rome, Paul wrote, "Whatsoever is not from faith is sin" (Rom. 14:23). Another translation reads, "Whatever is done

without a conviction of its approval by God is sinful" (*AMP*). Even another translation says, "Anyone who believes that something he wants to do is wrong shouldn't do it. He sins if he does, for he thinks it is wrong, and so for him it *is* wrong" (*TLB*). No matter what size a temptation is, if it doesn't feel right, chances are it isn't right.

4. **Would it cause another Christian to stumble in his or her faith?** Again, addressing the church in Rome, Paul wrote, "If your brother is distressed because of what you eat, you are no longer acting in love. Do not by your eating destroy your brother for whom Christ died. Do not allow what you consider good to be spoken of as evil" (Rom. 14:15-16, *NIV*). By giving in to a temptation, will you be doing something that could cause someone else to stumble spiritually? No man or woman lives and dies to himself or herself alone. What you do directly affects others, not only in this life but also in time and in eternity. This means that you need to not only live your life considering God's opinion, but you also need to be considerate of others.

Don't use your liberty to cause another person to stumble.

Are there any areas that are holding you back from fully committing yourself to Jesus Christ? Are you having so much fun that it's keeping you from God? Is any little pleasure really that good? Be honest. At least half of the time it is guilty pleasure at best, and a lot of times, it is not even that pleasurable.

FORGIVENESS WHEN YOU FAIL

If you do fail and give in to temptation—whether large or small—realize that your shortcomings and failures come as no surprise to God. David wrote, "O LORD, You have searched me and known me. You know my sitting down and my rising up; you understand my thought afar off. You comprehend my path and my lying down, and are acquainted with all my ways. For there is not a word on my tongue, but behold, O LORD, You know it altogether" (Ps. 139:1-4).

Maybe you have had a failure in your spiritual life recently. Maybe you have given in to a moral temptation. Maybe you have failed your spouse, children, coworkers or others who look up to you. Maybe you have fallen and wonder if you ever can be forgiven.

God can take our failures and turn them into successes. God can take losers and turn them into winners. For instance, in the Bible, we see how He took the failures in the life of one follower of Jesus, whose name was Simon Peter, and turned him into the foundation for the Church.

Like a Rock!

It is worth noting here how Simon got his new name, Peter. The disciples were with the Lord at a place called Caesarea Philippi when Jesus turned to them and said, "Who do men say that I am?" Various ideas were thrown out. Then Simon, under the inspiration of God Himself, said, "You are the Christ, the Son of the living God" (Matt. 16:16).

This was a remarkable moment. Peter had been given supernatural insight. Jesus told him, "I am giving you a new name. From this moment on, your name is Peter, and on this rock I will build my church" (see Matt. 16:17-18).

I wonder what the other disciples thought when Jesus gave Simon this new name. " 'Rock'? Is He on the level? Is this for real? You are calling *him* 'Rock'?" After all, when you think of a rock, you think of something that is solid. It implies dependability and an immovable nature. But Simon was far from that—at least at present. He was known to be at times hotheaded and impulsive. He was impetuous. To call Simon a rock almost seemed laughable.

This goes to show that God not only sees us for what we are, but He also sees us for who we can become. He sees our potential. We see a blank canvas, but God sees a finished painting. We see a lump of clay, but God sees a beautiful vase. We see problems, but God sees solutions. We see failures, but God sees successes. We see a Simon, but God sees a rock. In the same way, He sees us not only for who we are but also for who we can become. I once saw a funny bumper sticker that read, "Lord, help me to be the person my dog things I am." God wants to help us be the person that He knows we can be.

A Momentary Setback

In Peter's case, just as he began to live up to this new name, he had a serious lapse. He experienced a fall that was both notable and dramatic: Three times he denied that he ever knew Christ. You'll find the Gospel accounts of the story in Matthew 26:69-75, Mark 14:66-72, Luke 22:54-62 and John 18:15-27.

Yes, Peter fell. Yes, he had a lapse. But it was a temporary one. Later, in his own epistle, Peter wrote, "But may the God of all grace, who called us to His eternal glory by Christ Jesus, after you have suffered a while, perfect, establish, strengthen, and settle you" (1 Pet. 5:10). Peter was saying, "I know what I am talking about here. I have gone through hardship. I want you to know that God will get you through it."

In the same way, you have gone through certain experiences in your life. It might have been a tragedy. It might have been a mistake you made. It might have been giving in to one of those temptations that came in a small package. Maybe you've thought, *Why did the Lord let me go through these things? Why did God allow this to happen? Why didn't He protect me? Why did God allow me to fail?*

According to Scripture, God can cause "all things [to] work together for good" (Rom. 8:28). That does not necessarily mean that all things are in and of themselves good, but just that God can somehow bring some kind of good out of them. For instance, if you have experienced a personal tragedy, you can bring a measure of comfort to others who are going through the same situation and cannot see any light at the end of the tunnel. If you have given in to a temptation and paid the inevitable price, good can still come out of it if you are able to show another person why he or she should not consider giving in to that same temptation.

I could look back on my own childhood and say, "Lord, why did I have to be born into an alcoholic home? Why did I have to be in a home with a mother who was married and divorced seven times?" However, when I look back at the experiences I have had and the lessons that I have learned, I realize that God has used these things to help me reach out to others and have compassion for people who are going through similar situations.

Instead of being devastated by past failures or being upset with God as to why you went through certain things, ask God to take those things you have experienced and turn them into great lessons that you can share with others. God gives second chances. That is what He did for Peter. And that is what He can do for you.

FOR REFLECTION

Before you move on to chapter 4, I want to encourage you to apply what you've read here to your own life. Ponder the following questions and be honest with yourself as you try to answer. If possible, spend some time in reflective thought and prayer about these questions, asking God to point out areas in your life in which you need to rely on Him to help you.

1. When you're honest with yourself, what small temptations have you given in to during the course of your life?

2. Did these missteps and failures result in consequences that you had to face?

3. Would you consider these consequences as
   smaller or equal to the consequences that
   came with giving in to larger temptations?

3. Think of a temptation that you faced recently, or one that stands out from another
   time in your life. (Looking back at a past
   temptation will allow you to be more honest
   and objective than a temptation you are facing right now.) Ask yourself the four questions from the "Walking a Fine Line" section
   in this chapter:

   - Did the desire I had build me up spir-
     itually?
   - If I had given in to this temptation,
     would it have brought me under its
     power?
   - Did this desire feel wrong at the time?
     Did it give me an uneasy conscience?
   - By giving in to the temptation, would
     it have caused another Christian to
     stumble in his or her faith?

4. Can you think of times when God has used a failure or weakness in your life and turned it into a success for His kingdom? Reflect on how God used you in spite of your misstep.

5. Can you think of others who might be facing the same temptation that you gave in to? In what ways can your experience help them resist the temptation that is in front of them?

Don't you realize that friendship with this world makes you an enemy of God? I say it again, that if your aim is to enjoy this world, you can't be a friend of God. What do you think the Scriptures mean when they say that the Holy Spirit, whom God has placed within us, jealously longs for us to be faithful? He gives us more and more strength to stand against such evil desires.

JAMES 4:4-6, NLT

[Compromise] prompts us to be silent when we ought to speak for fear of offending. It prompts us to praise when it is not deserved, to keep people our friends. It prompts us to tolerate sin and not to speak out because to do so might give us enemies.

GRAHAM SCROGGIE

THE DANGER OF COMPROMISE

I once heard a story about a hunter who went deep into the woods in search of a bear. It seems that he wanted to shoot one and skin it for its coat. After a long wait, the hunter finally had a huge brown bear in his sight. Wrapping his finger slowly around the trigger and holding the barrel steady, he aimed for the center of the hulking animal's very large forehead.

Just as the hunter was preparing to squeeze the trigger, the bear turned around and, catching the hunter by surprise, said in a soft voice, "Wait! Let's talk this thing over! Isn't it better to talk than to shoot?"

The hunter was so surprised that he lowered his gun. The bear thanked him and said, "Now, what is it that you want? Can't we negotiate?"

"Well," the hunter replied, "actually, all I want is a fur coat!"

"Good," the bear said. "All I want is a meal!"

As the two sat down to negotiate, the hunter dropped his guard and laid his rifle down on a big, gray rock. Then the two went into the forest to talk. After a while, the bear came back out, alone. Apparently, the negotiations had been successful. The bear had a full stomach, and the hunter had his fur coat.

That's how "compromise" with temptation works.

Just as temptation can come in small packages, it can also come in the gray and fuzzy areas of life. In fact, the devil knows that one of the most effective ways to pull someone down is through the deadly, deceptive and effective ploy of compromise. Perhaps more people have been brought down by this strategy of his than any other. As a result, he keeps on using it.

LIVING IN TWO WORLDS

Have you ever heard the story of the guy who could not decide which side he wanted to fight for during the Civil War? He put on the coat of the North and the trousers of the South. And guess what? He got shot at from both sides! This is what happens to the compromiser, the person who tries to live in two worlds. It's a miserable place to be.

Sadly, there are many in the Church today who live a compromised life. The great British preacher G. Campbell

Morgan once said, "It is a remarkable thing that the church of Christ persecuted has been the church of Christ pure. On the other hand, the church of Christ patronized has been the church of Christ impure."

The Bible gives us an example in Revelation 2 of such a church—the church was Pergamos (see vv. 12-17), located in Pergamum, the capital of Asia Minor. Known for its rampant idolatry, Pergamum housed the altar of Zeus and was the center of Caesar worship. Idolatry, wickedness and sexual immorality were commonplace. The sin of the church at Pergamos was its toleration of evil, a sort of have-your-cake-and-eat-it-too philosophy.

Sadly, this is how most people want it today. They want to go to church—when they get around to it. They certainly want to go to heaven, but they still want to live in sin. They want to compromise by giving in to temptation, yet still not face any consequences. They want to party and commit immorality, lie when necessary, cheat if they have to, steal if it suits them, and hate and get revenge when someone else crosses them. They embrace the idea that they can sin to their heart's content, telling themselves that God will understand.

If you think you can sin to your heart's content without repercussions or that you can go out and break the commandments of God over and over because you're an exception to the rule, you are deceiving yourself.

I am not suggesting that Christians will not sin. The Bible clearly says, "If we say we have no sin, we deceive ourselves, and the truth is not in us" (1 John 1:8). But there is a big difference between the person who sins, is sorry for it and doesn't want to keep doing it and the person who continually, willfully, habitually sins over and over again and then says, "It is okay. God will forgive me."

The Bible says, "Shall we go on sinning so that grace may increase? By no means! We died to sin; how can we live in it any longer?" (Rom. 6:1-2, *NIV*). The devil introduced compromise into the church of Pergamos, and he will introduce such deception into the lives of people today.

If you look at the times in your life when you have fallen into sin, you could probably trace each instance back to a series of small compromises you made that led to the big compromise that led to your fall. As compromise finds its way into your life, it weakens you. You lose your effectiveness in this world. You lose your effectiveness as a Christian as well.

I am not suggesting that you be a holier-than-thou hypocrite. Instead, you should live in such a way that unbelievers could look at you and say, "There is something different about that person. Something that is desirable, something admirable." They may laugh at you at times, but deep in their hearts they usually deeply respect you. The person who lives in such a way has the power to reach people for the Kingdom. The compromising person, on the other hand, reaches no one.

Remember, Satan loves to use compromise as a mechanism for tempting us, because it means he's found a gray area in our lives in which he can confuse us. First, we compromise by giving in to a small temptation. As we compromise, it ultimately leads to immorality, idolatry and other sins.

Show me a person who is not living in close fellowship with God and I will show you a person who is on the way to bigger problems. It is only a matter of time. The best antidote to the temptations and compromises of this world is a passionate love relationship with Jesus Christ.

If there is a breakdown in your relationship with God, it is only a matter of time until compromises will start making their way into your life and until you start lowering your standards here and there. Keep your guard up. Stay close to Jesus. Let the fire of the first love burn brightly, and you will be strong.

THE ANATOMY OF COMPROMISE

Throughout Scripture, we see that one of the most effective strategies that Satan uses to tempt God's people is compromise. The biblical account of Moses and his confrontation with Pharaoh illustrates this struggle well.

God made it clear to Moses that he was to go to Pharaoh and demand the complete release of the Israelites, their children, their livestock and their possessions. There were to be no concessions, no compromises. This was the plan. God also told Moses that He would confirm His word with dramatic miracles to prove to Pharaoh that Moses had indeed been sent by God.

However, Moses' first meeting with Pharaoh was a disaster. Not only did Pharaoh refuse Moses' demand, but he also made the Israelites' burdens even worse than they had been before. In the same way, there will be times in your life when things will not be going so well, but you will be in the very will of God. That's when you must simply persist. You must get up and try again. That is what Moses did.

During Moses and Aaron's next visit to the court of Pharaoh, Aaron cast down his rod before Pharaoh and his servants, and the rod became a serpent. Pharaoh called his wise men and sorcerers, who imitated the miracle. But Aaron's rod swallowed up their rods, and Pharaoh's heart grew hard.

God then brought a series of 10 plagues, or judgments, on Egypt to bring Pharaoh to his senses. Each plague grew in intensity from the one before it. Yet Pharaoh's heart only grew harder. In fact, the more

Pharaoh saw, the harder his heart became.

Eventually, Pharaoh called for Moses and said that the Israelites could worship their God and sacrifice to Him, but they were to stay in Egypt. Moses refused. Okay, Pharaoh countered, but if you have to go, then don't go very far away.

Here we see the anatomy of a compromise. Just as Satan tried to get Moses to make a small concession in his situation, he will try to get you to make a small concession in the circumstances that you face. If you look at any time in your life when you have fallen into sin, I will guarantee that in every instance, if you retrace your steps, you will find that it started with a little bit of compromise.

"Go ahead, but don't go too far." See how subtle this is? It is not a complete denial of what you know is right, but it is a compromise nevertheless.

Moses refused to accept the compromise that Pharaoh proposed, and more plagues came. With plague after plague, Pharaoh began to wear down. He tried yet another concession, and Moses again refused. Finally, realizing that he didn't have any cards left to play, Pharaoh told Moses to go and worship the Lord, but to leave the flocks and herds behind.

Put yourself in Moses' sandals for a moment. Pharaoh was softening and giving in. Don't you think at that point you would have been tempted to say, "Who cares about the animals? Let's go. We are out of here. Pharaoh has released us."

But I love what Moses says: "Not a hoof shall be left behind" (Exod. 10:26). The point is, don't make deals with the devil. Whatever that deal is, it will ultimately lead to your undoing. When the devil comes and says, "You can believe in Jesus and go to church and read the Bible, but let me have this one little area of your life," don't let him have even one little thing. Like Moses, you must say, "You get zero, zip, nada. I have seen your agenda. I won't give you anything."

Maybe you are in a compromised state right now. If so, it's time to repent and make a clean break. And in the future, don't make any more deals with the devil. No more compromises. No more small concessions. Beware of the dangers of the compromised life.

FOR REFLECTION

Before you move on to chapter 5, I want to urge you to apply in your own life what you've read here. Ponder the following questions and be honest with yourself as you try to answer. If possible, spend some time in reflective thought and prayer about these questions.

Ask God to pinpoint areas in your life in which you need to rely on Him more to help you.

1. How would you define the word "compromise" when it comes to temptation?

2. Would you agree with the words I used to describe compromise—that it is a "deadly, deceptive and very effective ploy"? What other words would you add?

3. In what areas of your life has Satan tempted you to compromise?

4. What lies have you nearly believed regarding the lack of consequences you'll face if you give in to a compromising temptation?

5. Can you think of past times in your life when you made a series of smaller compromises that led to a major compromise and subsequent sin?

6. As you look back, what steps could you have taken to prevent the compromises you were making?

It was necessary for Jesus to be in every respect like us, his brothers and sisters, so that he could be our merciful and faithful High Priest before God. He then could offer a sacrifice that would take away the sins of the people. Since he himself has gone through suffering and temptation, he is able to help us when we are being tempted.

HEBREWS 2:17-18, *NLT*

Compromise is but the sacrifice of one right or good in the hope of retaining another—too often ending in the loss of both.

TRYON EDWARDS

JESUS FACES DOWN TEMPTATION

Maybe you've heard the story of the little boy in the grocery store. He's standing in the snack aisle, and on the shelf in front of him sits an open package of chocolate chip cookies. When a store employee approaches the boy and asks what he's doing, the boy replies, "Nothin'."

"Nothing?" asks the employee. "It looks to me like you're about to eat a cookie."

"You're wrong, mister. I'm trying *not* to eat a cookie."

In a nutshell (or a package of cookies), that's what temptation—and resisting it—is all about.

What makes resisting temptation difficult for many of us is that we don't want to discourage it completely. Like the little boy in the story, we want to be delivered from temptation, but we are unwilling to completely walk away from it. We pray against temptation, but then walk into places of vulnerability. The problem with this approach to temptation is that it is like thrusting one's fingers into a fire and praying they won't be burned!

Far too often, we're out of the will of God, essentially bringing temptation on ourselves. You might remember some of the steps that led to the fall of Simon Peter when he denied the Lord three times. The actual denial happened near the house of the High Priest of Israel, where Jesus was being examined on trumped-up charges. There, warming himself by the nearby fire from the chill of his soul, the denials began. Peter was outside of the will of God, and he had already taken other steps to make himself even more vulnerable, such as arguing with Jesus and not praying when the Lord told him to do so. He was just waiting for an accident to happen.

And it did.

When someone recognized Peter as one of the followers of Christ, his words of denial fell so quickly from his lips that it probably caused even him to shudder. How weak we are and prone to go the wrong way.

Like Eve before him, Peter was in the wrong place at the wrong time. This resulted in his doing the wrong thing. That's an explosive combination, and it will ultimately lead to a spiritual meltdown.

In chapter 1, we looked briefly at the story of how Satan tempted Jesus. Scripture tells us that Jesus "was led by the Spirit into the wilderness, being tempted for forty days by the devil" (Luke 4:1-2). Yet even though Jesus was facing a time of temptation, He was actually in the will of God. His experience provides an example that we can follow as we try *not* to give in to temptation.

ROUND 1: SATAN TAKES AIM

As we look at the three temptations of Jesus by Satan on the backside of a desolate wilderness, we see that they were directed toward three different areas of vulnerability. In the first temptation, turning stones to bread, Satan targeted Jesus physically. This was the temptation to place a physical drive before a spiritual need. We might call it, "Play now; pay later."

Satan said to Jesus, "If You are the Son of God, command this stone to become bread" (Luke 4:3). It's as if the devil was saying, "I was there at the Jordan . . . at Your baptism. What was that Your Father said? 'You are My beloved Son; in You I am well pleased.' Well, seeing that You are what You are, command these stones to become bread. C'mon, this should be easy for You."

Jesus shot back, "It is written, 'Man shall not live by bread alone, but by every word of God'" (v. 4). Essentially,

Christ was saying, "I'm not here as God to deal with you today. I'm here as a man to deal with you on man's behalf!" In other words, Jesus was giving us a template—an example or a model—for resisting temptation.

The enemy was saying, "Don't worry about the long-term repercussions of sin. Just enjoy the moment. Satisfy yourself! It can't be wrong if it feels so right. You deserve this. What happens in Vegas stays in Vegas!"

So many of us easily disregard—or at least temporarily set aside—the spiritual as we chase after the temporal pleasures this world has to offer. Only that cold, dead feeling that sin produces will bring us to our senses and back to the God we have wandered away from. In a sense, each and every day we all are faced with this very same temptation that Christ faced.

Each day, as His followers, we have a choice: Are we going to take the time to pray today, or will we choose to just ignore God? Are we going to look to Scripture to hear what the Lord might say to us, or are we going to read the newspaper instead? Are we going to do the right thing, or will we merely indulge ourselves if given the opportunity?

When we give in to temptations similar to this first temptation that Jesus faced, it's often not necessarily about sinning outright. Rather, it's about allowing the trivial to outweigh the more important matters, the temporary to overshadow the eternal, and the physical to become more important than the spiritual. We might put it this way: If a good thing takes the place of the best thing, it then becomes a bad thing.

Just as surely as we hunger for food each and every day, we need to have a hunger for God's Word, which will satisfy us so that we are no longer looking to this world to fulfill our deepest needs. Job summed it up this way: "I have not departed from the commandment of His lips; I have treasured the words of His mouth more than my necessary food" (Job 23:12).

ROUND 2: THE SHORTCUT

Frustrated with Jesus' resistance to his first temptation, Satan came with another that hit perhaps a bit closer to home: "Then the devil, taking Him up on a high mountain, showed Him all the kingdoms of the world in a moment of time. And the devil said to Him, 'All this authority I will give You, and their glory; for this has been delivered to me, and I give it to whomever I wish. Therefore, if You will worship before me, all will be Yours'" (Luke 4:5-7).

Jesus did not refute this bold assertion. He couldn't, because Satan was right. Although the devil is rightfully known as the father of lies, this time he was telling the truth. He really does have control of the kingdoms of this world—at least for now. When Adam sinned in the Garden, he forfeited paradise and this world to Satan, who is now "the god of this age" (2 Cor. 4:4). Satan is also called "the prince of the power of the air, the spirit who now works in the sons of disobedience" (Eph. 2:2).

This is why all attempts to reform this world, culture and society—apart from a change of heart that only the Holy Spirit can initiate—are ultimately futile.

Education won't do it.

Technology won't do it.

Politics won't do it.

Morality won't do it.

Even religion won't do it.

Only a life changed by Jesus Christ can bring about real and lasting change. Satan is primarily the one responsible for the gross perversion, the injustice, the rabid violence and the hate-fueled rebellion against God and His laws. Let me be bold: The devil has infiltrated politics, the media and much of organized religion.

But the clock is ticking for Satan. He knows his time is limited. A student of Scripture, he knows that his destruction is certain. The myth that he already rules hell—or will one day—is false. The fact of the matter is that he will be cast into hell to be tortured, as hell was created for the devil and his angels (see Matt. 25:41).

Of course, he would like to take as many people with him as possible. So for now, he is taking people captive to do his will (see 2 Tim. 2:26) and is blinding the minds of those who do not believe (see 2 Cor. 4:4).

A Fate Worse Than Death

As I said, Jesus did not refute Satan's claim that he could give Jesus control of the kingdoms of this world. But here's the point we don't want to miss about this second temptation the devil placed before Jesus: Satan was offering Jesus an opportunity to bypass the cross itself. Why would Satan do this? Because Jesus came to buy back that which had been forfeited in the Garden.

In the book of Revelation, which means "the unveiling," a dramatic scene unfolds. A book, clearly of the greatest significance, is produced in heaven, but no one is able to open it: "Then I saw a strong angel proclaiming with a loud voice, 'Who is worthy to open the scrolls and to loose its seals?' And no one in heaven or on the earth or under the earth was able to open the scroll, or to look at it. So I wept much, because no one was found worthy to open and read the scroll, or to look at it" (Rev. 5:2-4).

Suddenly, someone appears who can open the book. It's Jesus. The drama continues: "But one of the elders said to me, 'Do not weep. Behold, the Lion of the tribe of Judah, the Root of David, has prevailed to open the scroll and to loose its seven seals.' And I looked, and behold, in the midst of the throne and of the four living creatures, and in the midst of the elders, stood a Lamb as though it had been slain" (Rev. 5:5-6).

So what's going on here? How does this connect to Satan's temptation of Jesus in the wilderness? I believe that this book that only Jesus could open was—for all practical purposes—the "title deed" to the earth. Yes, it would be purchased back, but only at the highest cost anyone could ever pay: It would be bought back with the blood of Jesus. Jesus would have to suffer like no other before or after Him, for He Himself would bear all the sins of the entire human race: past, present and future.

For Jesus, that was a fate worse than death itself.

An Offer You Can't Refuse

So Satan was offering a deal. "I know why You have come, Jesus!" the devil was saying. "You have come back to purchase back that which was lost by Adam. Well, I'm going to make you an offer You can't refuse. I'll give it to You on a silver platter, if You like."

But there was a catch. A big one.

The devil said, "If You will give me the momentary pleasure of worshiping me, it will be Yours!"

Now, why would this offer be tempting to Jesus? Exactly because, as we mentioned, Satan was offering Jesus a way around the cross. We know that although the Lord willingly bore the cross, He clearly dreaded it. Everything in His humanity shrank from it. Remember, in the Garden of Gethsemane, "His sweat became like great drops of blood" (Luke 22:44). He cried out to the Father, "If it is Your will, take this cup away from Me; nevertheless not My will, but Yours, be done" (Luke 22:42). He prayed this same prayer three times!

Satan was now saying to Jesus, "Just bow once. Look at all You'll gain! Surely it's worth it. The ends justify the means! Think about it, Jesus. No Gethsemane. No scourging. No cross. And, most significantly, no bearing the sin of the world. Just bow before me."

Return Fire

Jesus did not, even for a moment, entertain such a wicked thought: "Jesus answered and said to him, 'Get behind Me, Satan! For it is written, "You shall worship the LORD your God, and Him only you shall serve"'" (Luke 4:8).

Notice that Satan said nothing about serving—he just wanted a moment of worship from Jesus. But the Lord recognized that just a moment of worship can easily mean a lifetime of service.

It always starts with the first time. We've all heard people say it, or perhaps we have even said it to ourselves:

"I'll only do it just this once."

"I'll know when to stop!"

"Besides, everybody's doing it."

Again, famous last words. You just reached a compromise with the hungry bear of temptation.

Just a Moment

Think about how many lives have been devastated by this twisted logic.

Just a moment at the altar of sexual promiscuity can lead to a lifetime of regret. That "one time" could lead to an unwanted pregnancy, a sexually transmitted disease or HIV/AIDS.

Just a moment at the altar of adultery could lead to a ruined marriage, a destroyed reputation and a devastated family, with ramifications for generations to come. That's how the devil works. Give him an inch and he'll want a mile. In fact, he'll take much more than a mile.

Just a moment at the altar of materialism could trigger an insatiable thirst for more and more. When you get that one thing—that one car, that one house, that one win at the gambling table—you think it will be enough. But somehow "enough" never happens. It never satisfies. It always has to be bigger and better, new and improved. The Bible says, "Hell and Destruction are never full; so the eyes of man are never satisfied" (Prov. 27:20).

Don't Bow at the Altar of Compromise

We looked at compromise in the previous chapter, but it's important to mention it again in the context of Satan's promise of the world to Jesus for just a moment of worship (and a lifetime of servitude). We don't know if Jesus thought back to the story of Shadrach, Meshach and Abed-Nego, who refused to compromise even when it meant saving their own lives, but we do know that Jesus knew the words and teachings of Scripture. At the very least, we can learn from the remarkable story of these three Jewish teenagers.

Through extraordinary circumstances, Shadrach, Meshach and Abed-Nego found themselves in positions of power and privilege under the mighty world ruler of that time, the king of Babylon. These young men would have been the envy of every teenager in the empire. In a sense, the world was their oyster.

As time passed, the deranged ruler of Babylon, Nebuchadnezzar, had an image erected of himself and commanded all his subjects, including these three young

Hebrews, to bow before it. But Shadrach, Meshach and Abed-Nego would have none of it. They knew that to bow—even for a moment—would be idolatrous and disobedient to their God.

Sure, they could have somehow justified it. They could have said, "When in Babylon, do as the Babylonians do!" Or they could have bowed and crossed their fingers behind their backs.

But these young men knew very well what was right and what was wrong. They also knew that what you worship for a moment you end up serving over the long haul. You probably already know how their story turned out. God delivered them from execution in the fiery furnaces of Babylon, and they were more blessed than ever.

Similarly, Satan offered Jesus "all the kingdoms of the world," and He refused. Yet others in the Bible sold out for so much less. Esau, for example, sold his birthright for a bowl of beans. He exchanged his entire spiritual future for the temporary physical gratification of a hot meal. At least, he could have bargained for a big, juicy steak!

A man named Achan forfeited his own life—as well as the lives of his family—for a chunk of gold and a Babylonian garment. And Judas sold his soul for 30 pieces of silver.

The problem with Satan, because he is the father of lies, is that he may offer you something and not deliver. You will lose out. Don't bow. Not for an instant. If you bow, you may end up worshiping. And God takes that very, very seriously.

ROUND 3: THE FINAL TEMPTATION

We come now to Satan's third temptation of Jesus: "Then he brought Him to Jerusalem, set Him on the pinnacle of the temple, and said to Him, 'If You are the Son of God, throw Yourself down from here. For it is written: "He shall give His angels charge over you, to keep you," and, "In their hands they shall bear you up, lest you dash your foot against a stone"'" (Luke 4:9-11).

What happened here? Did the devil get religion? This was Satan himself quoting Scripture. Yet it's very important to note that as he quoted from Psalm 91, he left out something. The passage he was quoting, Psalm 91:11-12, says, "For He shall give His angels charge over you, to keep you in all your ways. In their hands they shall bear you up, lest you dash your foot against a stone."

If Satan intentionally left out something, then I want to know why, don't you? The very fact that he omitted something indicates just how important the missing words must have been to a correct understanding of the text. And here is the phrase that comes up missing in Satan's recitation of Psalm 91: "to keep you in all your ways" (v. 11).

"Your ways"? Whose ways? This passage, as Satan knew full well, does not refer to paths of our own personal choosing. In context, it clearly refers to God's ways. Once you leave God's ways, you void—for all practical purposes—the promises found in the rest of this powerful psalm that range from God's protection to His provision.

In other words, we cannot intentionally disobey God, flagrantly violate His Word, and still expect His blessing of angelic protection and provision. Sometimes, God graciously delivers us from a situation that has come about as a result of our own disobedience. But if we then return to the same or a similar situation, consoling ourselves with the hope that God will once again get us out of this mess, we're only deceiving ourselves.

Don't confuse God's grace with His approval. Just because He graciously forgives a sin we commit again and again does not mean that He has changed His mind and now approves of that sin. The Bible tells us, "When the sentence for a crime is not quickly carried out, the hearts of the people are filled with schemes to do wrong" (Eccles. 8:11, *NIV*).

You cannot expect to be preserved if you follow sinful ways! We are to trust the Lord, not test Him.

FOR REFLECTION

Before you move on to chapter 6, I want to encourage you to apply to your own life what you've read about the temptations that Jesus faced. Ponder the following questions and be honest with yourself as you answer. Spend some time in reflective thought and prayer, asking God to point out areas in your life in which you need to rely on Him to help you with the temptations you face.

1. In case you missed the verse at the beginning of the chapter, let me repeat it here:

    It was necessary for Jesus to be in every respect like us, his brothers and sisters, so that he could be our merciful and faithful High Priest before God. He then could offer a sacrifice that would take away the sins of the people. Since he himself has gone through suffering and temptation, he is able to help us when we are being tempted (Heb. 2:17-18, *NLT*).

Now, look back at each temptation in Luke 4 and notice how Jesus resisted these temptations. Did He use His deity to resist Satan's lures?

2. What methods that Jesus used of resisting temptation can you use in your own life?

3. Which of the three temptations that Jesus faced hits closest to home for you? Why?

4. Do you most often face temptations involving what or who you worship, material pleasures, or your safety and security? Why do you think the father of lies frequently tempts you in that particular area?

5. What steps can you take to avoid temptations in that area?

6. What needs do you have in that area that you should rely on the certain promises of God— not some hollow promise from Satan—to satisfy?

How precious are your thoughts about me, O God! They are
innumerable! I can't even count them; they outnumber the
grains of sand! And when I wake up in the morning, you are
still with me! Search me, O God, and know my heart; test
me and know my thoughts. Point out anything in me that
offends you, and lead me along the path of everlasting life.

PSALM 139:17-18,23-24, *NLT*

He will be with you also, all the way, that faithful God.
Every morning when you awaken to the old and tolerable
pain, at every mile of the hot uphill dusty road of tiring duty,
on to the judgment seat, the same Christ there as ever,
still loving you, still sufficient for you, even then.
And then, on through all eternity.

THOMAS À KEMPIS

MOVING FORWARD

You might remember some time ago when the excitable Steve Irwin of *Crocodile Hunter* fame held his infant in one arm while using his other hand to feed a rather large croc a piece of raw meat. There was a great public outcry as people wondered why Irwin would take such a needless risk. Irwin's response was that he wanted to get his child "croc savvy."

Of course, the problem was that with one stumble, Steve's baby could easily have been a croc snack. When asked about the danger of this, he said, "It's all about perceived danger; I was in complete control. People say, 'Well, what if you had fallen?' But for that to take place a meteorite would have had to come out of the sky and hit Australia at 6.6 on the Richter scale."[1]

My question is, Why take a risk like that? Why push it? In the same way, we should never, ever lower our guard or think we are somehow immune or temptation proof. What a dangerous attitude that is! Just when we feel the most secure within ourselves—when we are convinced that our spiritual life is at its strongest, our doctrine is the soundest, our morals the purest and our lives the most stable—that is when we should be most alert to danger and most dependent on our Lord. When we think we've reached some spiritual plateau is when we may find ourselves in deadly jeopardy.

STRONG MEN WITH BIG WEAKNESSES

In chapter 1, we talked about who temptation comes to and when it comes. We mentioned that new believers often face temptation and that temptation often comes to all of us during times when we experience great blessing.

In addition, sometimes the weakest Christian is not in as much danger as the strongest one. This is because our strongest virtues can also be our greatest vulnerabilities. In fact, many of the great personalities of the Bible experienced times of vulnerability. Take the following very human examples of this:

Moses, the great lawgiver, was known as the meekest man on the face of the earth, yet pride and presumption dealt him a fatal blow.

Samson, the great judge of Israel and a man of supernatural strength, fell because he yielded to his natural desires.

The miracle-working prophet Elijah, distinguished throughout his ministry by his great boldness and faith, was paralyzed by fear that dropped him into a deep depression.

As we already discovered, Simon Peter, who considered himself the Lord's strongest and most loyal companion in times of danger, melted like an ice cube on a hot sidewalk when confronted by a young girl.

We must never rest on our laurels. There will always be new mountains to climb, new obstacles to overcome and, yes, more temptations to resist. The mature believer realizes that there is always a long way to go. He or she never forgets our human potential and propensity for sin.

JUST A LITTLE BIT WON'T HURT, WILL IT?

None of us is immune to temptation, yet we have a tendency to think that we are. Do any of these statements sound familiar?

"Oh, I can handle a little marijuana. It won't be a problem."

"One drink won't hurt!"

"Just a little porn can't be all that bad. I won't do it again."

"A little flirting is fun. What's the harm?"

Famous last words. Speaking of which, have you ever heard the last words of Bucky O'Neill?

Bucky O'Neill was an Arizona lawyer, miner, cowboy, gambler, newspaperman, sheriff and congressman who rode into battle as one of Teddy Roosevelt's famous Rough Riders during the Spanish-American War. Moments prior to the famous charge up Kettle Hill, O'Neill was standing up, smoking a cigarette and joking with his troops while under withering fire from the ridge. One of his sergeants shouted to him above the noise, "Captain, a bullet is sure to hit you!"

O'Neill shouted back, "Sergeant, there isn't a Spanish bullet made that will kill me." No sooner had O'Neill uttered those words than he was hit and killed by a Spanish bullet.

The lesson here is that no one is bulletproof . . . or temptation proof. This brings us to my next point: Never lower your guard. Always go forward spiritually.

I once heard the story of a young captain who served in the ranks of Napoleon's army. When the captain was recommended for a military promotion, Napoleon asked why this particular man had been suggested.

His commanding officer answered, "Well, out on the battlefield several days ago, he displayed unusual courage and, as a result, a victory was won."

"Good," Napoleon replied. "What did he do the next day?"

We might talk about what we did for the Lord 10 weeks ago or 10 years ago. But what did we do the next day? What about today? Are we preparing for tomorrow? We can't live in the past. Our relationship with Christ should be flourishing and growing. It requires constant maintenance and cultivation.

As the Bible exhorts us, "But you, dear friends, must continue to build your lives on the foundation of your holy faith. And continue to pray as you are directed by the Holy Spirit. Live in such a way that God's love can bless you as you wait for the eternal life that our Lord Jesus Christ in his mercy is going to give you" (Jude 1:20-21, NLT).

The day we stop being built up on the foundation of our faith is the day our faith will begin the process of breaking down. Scripture reminds us that God's mercies are new every morning (see Lam. 3:23) and that we must take up our cross daily and follow Him (see Luke 9:23).

We must always be moving forward spiritually. If we fail to do this, we will become sitting ducks, more vulnerable than ever to the enticements and temptations of the devil. Although it has been said many times, it's still true: The best defense is a good offense. The best way not to go backward is to keep going forward.

Let's not be satisfied with what we did for Christ once upon a time. Let's not preoccupy ourselves with old newspaper clippings that recount our victories and mountaintop experiences. Let's press forward and follow Him.

FOR REFLECTION

Before you move on to chapter 7, I want to encourage you to apply what you've read in this brief but important chapter to your own life. Ponder the following questions and be honest with yourself as you answer. Ask God to point out areas in your life in which you need to rely on Him to help you with moving forward so you don't become spiritually stagnant.

1. James 4:7 states, "Resist the devil and he will flee from you." How do you think that staying active in your faith can help you resist Satan and his temptations?

2. In this chapter, I stated that our strongest virtues can also be our greatest vulnerabilities. Think about your own life and what you and others have identified as your greatest skills and abilities. In what ways might those virtues be areas of temptation for you?

3. Often, we rely on our own areas of strength and neglect surrendering those areas to God's control. How might holding on to control result in temptation in your areas of greatest strength?

4. How can you steel yourself against falling into temptation in these areas?

5. Look at some of the excuses listed in the "Just a Little Bit Won't Hurt, Will It?" section. Did you recognize yourself in any of these phrases?

6. What other "famous last words" have you uttered or heard others state that you could add to this list?

*All Scripture is inspired by God and is useful to teach us what
is true and to make us realize what is wrong in our lives.
It straightens us out and teaches us to do what is right.
It is God's way of preparing us in every way, fully equipped
for every good thing God wants us to do.*

2 TIMOTHY 3:16-17, *NLT*

*You choose to go voluntarily into the fire. The blaze might
well destroy you. But if you survive, every blow of the
hammer will serve to shape your being. Every drop of water
wrung from you will temper and strengthen your soul.*

MARGARET WEIS

Note
1. Associated Press, "Crocodile Hunter Stirs Scandal with Baby
   Stunt," *CTV.ca*, January 3, 2004. http://www.ctv.ca/servlet/
   ArticleNews/story/CTVNews/1073090900773_57/?hub=Ent
   ertainment%204 (accessed February 8, 2005).

WEAPONS FOR BATTLING TEMPTATION

Jack Handey, known for his odd sense of humor frequently expressed on old *Saturday Night Live* programs in a segment titled "Deep Thoughts," wrote an equally odd book entitled *Fuzzy Memories*. In it, Handey relates the story of a bully who demanded his lunch money every day when he was a child. Because Handey was smaller than the bully, he simply gave the bully his money.

"Then I decided to fight back," Handey continues. "I started taking karate lessons, but the instructor wanted $5 a lesson. That was a lot of money. I found that it was cheaper to pay the bully, so I gave up karate."[1]

Unfortunately, many Christians have the same attitude about Satan and the temptations that come their way. It's easier to pay the bully than learn how to fight him.

TEMPTATION RESISTANT: GOD'S WORD

In chapter 5, we looked at the three temptations that Satan presented to Jesus in the wilderness. You might recall that Jesus knew what weapon to use to defeat each temptation. In each of the three temptations, we see that Jesus used the weapon of the Word of God.

In each of those critical moments of temptation, Jesus was "rightly dividing the word of truth" (see 2 Tim. 2:15). Rather than exercising executive privilege (which He could have done because He was God), Jesus gave us the model of winning spiritual battles with the Word of God and in the power of the Holy Spirit. What Jesus did to resist Satan's temptations, we can do. Our primary weapon is the same weapon Jesus wielded in the wilderness: God's powerful, unchanging Word.

In Ephesians 6, the apostle Paul likens the Christian life to a spiritual battle and warns us to arm ourselves. Using a metaphor that people of his time would have been very familiar with, Paul drew an analogy from the armor of a Roman soldier (these guys were everywhere). Along with the various pieces of spiritual armor that Paul mentions, such as the belt of truth, the shield of faith and the helmet of salvation, he also speaks of "the sword of the Spirit, which is the word of God" (Eph. 6:17). All the other pieces of armor are defensive with the exception of this sword, which is both a defensive and an offensive weapon.

This is important to note, because you don't attack an enemy with your helmet or shield. You attack with an offensive weapon—a sharp sword. In the same way, the primary weapon for prevailing over temptation is the sword of the Spirit—the very Word of God, the Bible. As a believer, if you do not have a good working knowledge of Scripture, then you will more easily become a casualty in the spiritual battle.

USE IT OR LOSE IT

Sometimes, people ask me to sign their Bibles, and when I do, I often write these words: "Sin will keep you from this book, and this book will keep you from sin." Satan will do everything he can to keep you from God's Word. That's just what he did with Eve in the very first temptation ever recorded. He first questioned what God had said, then distorted it, and finally added to it.

Success or failure in the Christian life depends on how much of the Bible we get into our hearts and minds on a regular basis as well as on how obedient we are to what God's Word says. If we neglect the study of the Scripture, our spiritual life will ultimately unravel, because everything we need to know about God and living as a believer is taught in the Bible. And if it can't be found in the pages of Scripture, you don't need it.

Some people say that they need more than the Bible. They claim to receive new revelations from God. But we need to realize that if it's new, it's not true. And if it's true, then it's not new.

We often forget what we ought to remember and remember what we ought to forget. That's why every believer must make it a top priority to not only know the Word of God, but also to memorize it. To this day, my brain holds memory banks filled with obscure song lyrics, old television commercials and other trivial, mostly useless information. How much better it would be to have those memory banks filled with God's eternal, life-giving Word!

CARRY IT IN YOUR HEART

We need to make a conscious effort to keep the Word of God at the forefront of our hearts and minds. While it's good to carry a Bible in our briefcase, pocket or purse, the best place to carry God's Word is in our heart.

In Deuteronomy, God commanded His people to "Lay up these words of mine in your heart and in your soul. . . . You shall teach them to your children, speaking of them when you sit in your house, when you walk by the way, when you lie down, and when you rise up" (11:18-19).

Once select verses of Scripture have been grafted into your memory, they will become a powerful resource to you for the rest of your life. You will never regret the time you have invested in downloading God's own words into your mind. There will be times when those verses, passages and chapters you have learned will pay amazing dividends. Memorized Scripture will bring comfort and peace to your heart in times of great pressure or sorrow and will provide you with strength to stand in times of intense temptation. As the psalmist said, "Your word I have hidden in my heart, that I might not sin against You" (Ps. 119:11). And Psalm 37 tells us, "The law of his God is in his heart; none of his steps shall slide" (v. 31).

As the days of your life slip by, you must use what you know. Your mind should be so saturated with God's Word that it functions like a spiritual computer, enabling you to remember relevant verses when you find yourself under attack from the dark side. It is the ministry of the Holy Spirit to bring God's Word to your mind when you need it. Jesus said, "But the Helper, the Holy Spirit, whom the Father will send in My name,

He will teach you all things, and bring to your remembrance all things that I said to you" (John 14:26). However, the Spirit of God will not necessarily remind you of something you haven't learned.

So let me ask you: What shape is your sword in? Is it polished from daily use as you study the Scripture on a regular basis? Is it sharpened on the anvil of experience as you have applied and obeyed its truth in your life? Or has it become rusty from lack of preparation or dulled by disobedience?

BUT, I'M NOT GOD!

You might be saying, "Greg, of course Jesus could quote God's Word and use it to resist Satan's temptations. After all, Jesus was and is God!"

While that's true, it's even more important to remember that Satan is *not* God. Certainly, we should never underestimate the devil. He is a sly and skillful adversary with many years' experience in dealing with humanity. He is a powerful foe. Yet he can be overcome. Let's examine some facts about Satan.

Satan :

Powerful, But Not Divine

When you face temptation, you need to keep in mind that Satan is nowhere near to being the equal of God.

God is omnipotent (all-powerful), omniscient (all-knowing) and omnipresent (present everywhere). The devil, in sharp contrast, does not possess these divine attributes. Certainly, Satan is very powerful—more powerful than any man and more powerful than most angels. But he is not anywhere near to being the equal of God.

Satan's knowledge is limited. He can't know all of your thoughts. And while God can be everywhere at the same time, Satan can be in only one place at one time. However, he does not work alone. He has his minions demon forces that do his dirty work (see Eph. 6:10-12).

Can Do Nothing Without Permission

Just as important, you need to remember that Satan can do nothing in the life of a Christian without God's permission. While God may allow demonic attacks in your life, you are still under His divine protection. In the book of Job, for example, we read of the angels coming to present themselves before the Lord. Satan was among them, and God said to him, "From where do you come?" (Job 1:7). Satan answered, "From going to and fro on the earth, and from walking back and forth on it." Then the Lord essentially began bragging on Job, who was "a blameless and upright man" (v. 8). Satan, in response, pointed out the hedge of protection God had placed around Job's household and everything he owned (see v. 10).

This passage shows that in spite of the devil's power and wicked agenda, he must ask permission when it comes to influencing the life of the child of God, because God has placed a divine hedge of protection around His own. You can be oppressed to some degree, but if you are a Christian, neither the devil nor a demon can ever take control of your life. When you placed your faith in Jesus Christ, you came under His protection. He placed an I.D. tag on you that said, "Property of Jesus Christ. Bought with the Blood." Satan knows this and must back off.

Having said that, this doesn't mean that the devil can't try to lure you out of God's protection and draw you into his web of deception. The day you put your faith in Jesus Christ, your eternal address changed from a place known as hell to a place called heaven. It was a day in which you passed from darkness to light, a day in which you found new purpose and meaning. It was also a day in which a very real spiritual war began in your life. Conversion made your heart a battlefield. You came to realize that not only is there a God who loves you, but there is also a devil who hates you and wants to pull you back into your old ways again.

That's why, as a child of God, your objective should be to stay as close to the Lord as you possibly can—and keep as much distance between yourself and the devil as possible.

Accuser of the Brethren

The devil wants to pull you down before God. Then he wants to accuse you. On more than one occasion, the Scriptures refer to Satan as an accuser. Revelation 12:10 calls him "the accuser of our brethren, who accused them before our God day and night."

Satan wants you to believe that you are not worthy to approach God. But you need to remember that you are not approaching God on the basis of your worthiness. You are approaching God on the basis of what Jesus did for you at the cross. Remember that, because the devil doesn't want you to know it. He wants to accuse you before God and keep you away from Him.

Sometimes, such as when you are feeling guilty about giving in to a temptation, you may struggle to distinguish between Satan's accusations and the Holy Spirit's conviction. Let me tell you the difference: Satan will always try to drive you away from the Cross, while the Holy Spirit will always bring you back to it.

Has Already Lost

You also need to remember that the devil was soundly defeated at the Cross of Calvary. Speaking of what Jesus accomplished at the cross, the apostle Paul writes, "Having disarmed principalities and powers, He made a public spectacle of them, triumphing over them in it" (Col. 2:15). This means that each of us can be set free by the power of Jesus Christ.

FOR REFLECTION

Before you move on to the final chapter of this book, I want to encourage you to apply what you've read here to your own life. Ponder the following questions and be honest with yourself as you answer. Again, I encourage you to spend some time in reflective thought and prayer, asking God to point out areas in your life in which you need to rely on Him to help you use the weapons He has provided to battle temptations.

1. On a piece of paper, personalize 2 Timothy 3:16-17 (*NLT*) as follows:

    > All Scripture is inspired by God and is useful to teach [your name] what is true and to make [your name] realize what is wrong in my life. It straightens me out and teaches me to do what is right. It is God's way

of preparing [your name] in every way, fully equipped for every good thing God wants me to do.

Spend some extended time in prayer, asking God to help you make this promise true in your life.

2. If you need to spend more time studying and memorizing Scripture, ask God to help you find the time and to have the discipline to do it. If you need to spend more time applying and living out what Scripture teaches, ask God to provide more opportunities for you to do that. Ask the Holy Spirit to help you identify activities that tend to pull you away from the Lord instead of drawing you closer to Him.

3. What divine qualities or attributes have you mistakenly given to Satan? Use a Bible dictionary or search online to create a list of God's attributes. I mentioned some in the "But, I'm Not God!" section of this chapter: God is all-powerful; God is all-knowing; God is present everywhere.

4. Read Job 1:6-22. What do you note about Satan's limitations when he wants to tempt one of God's followers? What do you note about the ways God protects His followers from Satan?

We have a great High Priest who has gone to heaven, Jesus the Son of God. Let us cling to him and never stop trusting him. This High Priest of ours understands our weaknesses, for he faced all of the same temptations we do, yet he did not sin. So let us come boldly to the throne of our gracious God. There we will receive his mercy, and we will find grace to help us when we need it.

HEBREWS 4:14-16, *NLT*

Fundamentally, our Lord's message was Himself. He did not come merely to preach a Gospel; He himself is that Gospel. He did not come merely to give bread; He said, "I am the bread." He did not come merely to shed light; He said, "I am the light." He did not come merely to show the door; He said, "I am the door." He did not come merely to name a shepherd; He said, "I am the shepherd." He did not come merely to point the way; He said, "I am the way, the truth, and the life."

J. SIDLOW BAXTER

Note
1. Jack Handey, *Fuzzy Memories* (Kansas City, MO: Andrews and McNeel, 1996), n.p.

Jesus: The Ultimate Weapon Against Temptation

A couple of years ago, my son Jonathan was taking scuba diving lessons. He had been trained for a few hours on the previous day, and now it was time for the scuba instructor to take him out for an actual dive. I had been certified as a scuba diver for about 10 years, so I decided to go along with them.

As we went to get into the boat and go out for the dive, we noticed that the water was pretty choppy. Jonathan was a little nervous about the whole thing. It had been calm the day before, and he had done most of his practicing in the swimming pool. Now we were going into the real ocean, where the waters were turbulent. The waters were so rough that it was a little frightening. As we began our descent, I could see the panic in Jonathan's eyes.

I didn't know what to do because, quite frankly, I was feeling a little frightened myself! But the instructor handled it perfectly. He said to Jonathan, "Look at me right now." Jonathan looked at him. He said, "Remember your training? This is what you do." The instructor calmed him down. Jonathan put in his regulator, and we went under the water. Immediately, everything was calm and beautiful, and we were fine.

We need to do the same thing when we face storms and temptations in our lives. We simply need to look to our Instructor, Jesus. He is saying, "Look at Me. Don't worry about the waves. Don't worry about the circumstances. Don't panic about the temptations. Remember your training!"

BAD NEWS FOR THE DEVIL

During the Korean War, enemy forces were advancing on a military unit known as the Baker Company. This unit had been cut off from the rest of the regiment, and for several hours, despite repeated attempts to communicate, no word had been heard from it. Finally, headquarters picked up a faint signal. Straining to hear each word, the radio operator asked, "Baker Company, do you read me?"

"This is Baker Company" was the reply.

"Baker Company, what is your situation?"

"The enemy is to the east of us. The enemy is to the west of us. The enemy is to the north of us. The enemy is to the south of us . . . and we are not going to let them escape this time!"

That is the kind of attitude we ought to have as believers. But sometimes we find ourselves in the same dilemma as the Baker Company: The enemy is to the north of us, to the south of us, to the east of us and to the west of us. Everywhere we look, we see the devil's dirty work. It can be overwhelming. We begin to think, *What's the use?*

We can't let that happen. We must have faith and say, "We can move forward. God can work through our lives." We need to be active in the work of the Lord. The devil is active in his work, because he recognizes that his time is short.

Even if some people in the world don't believe it, Satan knows that Jesus is coming back very soon. Therefore, the devil is stepping up his efforts. The return of the Lord is bad news for the devil, but it is good news for the Church. For Satan, it is an incentive to attack our faith and try to make us stumble and fall. For us, it is an incentive to share our faith and live holy lives.

Simply put, the devil does not want us to follow Jesus Christ. He did everything he could to keep us from coming to Christ in the first place, and now he wants to do everything he can to keep us immobilized and ineffective for the kingdom of God. But here is what it comes down to: If we are Christians, there is no room for spiritual pacifism, because we will become a spiritual casualty. If we are Christians, we are going to be in a battle.

The real question is, Will we advance or retreat? We can either stay in the wilderness or we can enter the Promised Land. In the Christian life, either we are overcomers, or we will be overcome. God has brought us out of a life of sin and bondage to bring us into the life of power and victory in which we are serving the Lord.

THE BATTLE IS WON!

Here's a foundational truth to remember about temptation: Yes, there is a battle in our daily lives, but the battle has already been won by Jesus Christ at the cross. The choice we have to make is whether or not we will walk and live in that victory.

Prior to His crucifixion, Jesus said, "Now is the judgment of this world; now the ruler of this world will be cast out" (John 12:31). Referring to this same event on Calvary, Hebrews tells us, "Inasmuch then as the children have partaken of flesh and blood, He Himself likewise shared in the same, that through death He might destroy him who had the power of death, that is, the devil" (Heb. 2:14). The apostle Paul reminds us that God "canceled the record that contained the charges against us. He took it and destroyed it by nailing it to Christ's cross" (Col. 2:14, NLT).

Maybe you're wondering, *If Jesus' death at Calvary was powerful and complete, then why is Satan still on the scene, doing his dirty work?* It's because God has allowed it. That isn't a cop-out. It is simply recognition of a temporary situation.

Remember, the enemy does nothing in the life of the Christian without the express permission of God. Jesus said to Peter, "Indeed, Satan has asked for you, that he may sift you as wheat. But I have prayed for you" (Luke 22:31-32). In the same way that Jesus prayed for Peter, the Lord is praying for us, too.

We touched on this in the previous chapter, but I want to stress again that every temptation that comes our way has to go through God's protective grid. Satan has to ask God's permission before he can tempt us.

In this fallen and broken world of ours, God allows temptation. In His amazing sovereignty, He can even use that temptation to strengthen us spiritually and draw us closer to Himself. But God will never allow more temptation in our lives than we can handle. He will always provide a way of escape so that we'll be able to bear it and come through on the victory side (see 1 Cor. 10:13). That's His promise.

However, if you're not a Christian—if you have never made a commitment to Jesus Christ—then you don't have this promise from God. You won't be able to resist temptation effectively. You will be vulnerable to Satan's attacks, his manipulation, and even his possession.

But God loved you so much that 2,000 years ago, He sent His Son to die on the cross for every sin you have ever committed. At the cross, Jesus dealt a decisive blow against Satan and his demons. The person who puts his or her faith in Jesus Christ no longer has to be afraid of what the devil will do, because Scripture says, "He who is in you is greater than he who is in the world" (1 John 4:4).

Is Christ living inside of you? When temptation comes knocking on my door, I like to say, "Lord, would You mind answering that?" I don't want to mess with it. I don't want to go one-on-one with evil desires. It's too much for me. So I ask the Lord to help me, protect me and strengthen me. And He does.

But if you're not a Christian, you're on your own. And that's a bad place to be.

Maybe as you read these words, you find yourself in the throes of some addiction. You've tried to get out. You need to say, "Lord, I'm a sinner. Come into my heart and help me."

Maybe you once made a commitment to Christ, but at some point you walked away from the commitment, and you have been living in disobedience. You find yourself trying to live in two worlds, and it's tearing you apart. God knows all about it. Go to Him and say, "Lord, I'm sick of pretending. I'm weary to death of lying to myself and closing my eyes to the real condition of my life. Help me, God. Get me out of this. I want to live for You."

If you have never come to Jesus or you need to come back to Jesus, then why don't you do that today?

GRABBING HOLD OF THE HOPE

Let me conclude by saying that Satan isn't called the father of lies for no reason. When he says that you will get away with something, he's lying to you. You won't get away with it.

You are not the sole exception to the Scripture that says, "Do not be deceived, God is not mocked; for whatever a man sows, that he will also reap" (Gal. 6:7), or the verse that warns, "Be sure your sin will find you out" (Num. 32:23). If you sin, it will come out sooner or later. Just because you got away with it yesterday and might be getting away with it today doesn't mean you will get away with it tomorrow. You need to say, "Lord, I know this is wrong. I am coming to You in humility and repentance and asking You to forgive me as I turn from this sin."

If you persist along your path of disobedience, your sin will eventually catch up with you. When it does, you really have no idea of what sort of consequences you'll be facing. That's why you need to stop now, make a U-turn in your thinking, and come back to God.

Why else would God have had you read this little book? This could be His warning to you at this very moment. He might be saying to you, "I know what you are doing. You know what you are doing. You need to deal with this. You need to stop. And you need to stop now!

I believe the person who is willing to say, "I have not come as far as I want to. I need to move forward, grow, learn and stretch. I have so much ahead of me to live for in the Lord. I want to go after it—I want to build myself up" is the kind of person who will have a good, strong spiritual life.

That doesn't mean he or she will have a problem-free life. None of us gets a free pass when it comes to the hurts, hassles and heartaches of this world. None of us is exempt from setbacks and temptations. But the person who seeks the Lord will be a person who moves forward in power.

On the other hand, for the person who is just trying to hang on, who is not learning and growing, and who toys with temptation, it will be only a matter of time until he or she will go down in defeat.

Which person are you going to be? Make that determination right now. Decide ahead of time. Will you be another victim of temptation, or will you become a victor? Will you be conquered, or will you be more than a conqueror? It's up to you.

The apostle Paul wrote, "No, dear brothers and sisters, I am still not all I should be, but I am focusing all my energies on this one thing: Forgetting the past and looking forward to what lies ahead, I strain to reach the end of the race and receive the prize for which God, through Christ Jesus, is calling us up to heaven" (Phil. 3:13-14, *NLT*).

If you need to make a commitment or recommitment to Jesus Christ, why not do it right now?

Here is a suggested prayer:

Lord Jesus, I know that I am a sinner. But I believe that You died on the cross for my sins and paid the price for every wrong I have ever done. I turn from that sin right now and ask You to be my Savior, my Lord, my God and my Friend. Help me to resist temptation and walk in Your will from this moment forward. Thank You for hearing this prayer, and that I am now forgiven. I pray these things in the name of Jesus, amen.

If you prayed this prayer, I would like to hear from you! You can write me at Greg Laurie, c/o Harvest Ministries, 6115 Arlington Avenue, Riverside, California, 92504. Or you can contact me by e-mail at Greg@harvest.org. You can also visit our website at www. harvest.org to learn more about following Christ.

FOR REFLECTION

We've ended each chapter in this book with a section of reflective questions. My goal has been to encourage you to apply what you've read here to your own life. As we close the book, I again urge you to ponder the following questions and be honest with yourself as you answer. You can write the answers down, or you can simply spend some time in reflective thought and prayer.

1. Think back to the times when you've felt surrounded by Satan's temptations. What

have you read in this chapter (and through-out the book) that helps you know that you can overcome the temptations, no matter how desperate the situation seems?

2. Why do you think God allows Satan to tempt us?

3. When you're facing temptation, what do the following words of Scripture mean to you: "Let us come boldly to the throne of our gracious God. There we will receive his mercy, and we will find grace to help us when we need it" (Heb. 4:16, *NLT*)?

4. Have you invited Christ to be your Savior? When temptation comes knocking on your door, are you able to say, "Jesus, would You mind answering that?"

5. Finally, I encourage you to reread the "Grabbing Hold of the Hope" section in this chapter. Decide whether you want to be a victim of temptation or a victor over temptation, and then make a full-fledged commitment to Jesus Christ.

ABOUT THE AUTHOR

Greg Laurie, senior pastor of Harvest Christian Fellowship in Riverside, California, began his pastoral ministry at age 19 by leading a Bible study of 30 people, which God has since transformed into a congregation that is among the eight largest churches in America. In 1990, Greg began holding public evangelistic events called Harvest Crusades. Since then, nearly three million people have attended Harvest Crusades across the United States and in Australia. Greg is the featured speaker on the nationally syndicated radio program *A New Beginning*, heard nationwide and overseas. He is also the featured host of the television program *Harvest: Greg Laurie*, which is seen internationally. He is the author of a number of books, including the Gold Medallion-Award winner *The Upside-Down Church*. In addition, Greg has authored the study notes for two *New Living Translation* study Bibles. He and his wife, Cathe, have two children and live in Southern California.

Greg Laurie
Harvest Ministries
6115 Arlington Avenue
Riverside, CA 92504
Greg@Harvest.org
www.harvest.org

Also From Greg Laurie

Renowned pastor and evangelist Greg Laurie helps unravel some of the mystery surrounding end-times events as he examines what the Bible has to say about life in the last days and explores topics such as:

- Important signs of the last days
- The difference between the Rapture and the Second Coming
- Israel's significance in end-times events
- America's mysterious absence in Bible prophecy
- Life during the Tribulation period

Are These the Last Days? will help you take some of the guesswork out of understanding the last days and will encourage you to live confidently and expectantly in an uneasy and uncertain world.

Are These the Last Days?
How to Live Expectantly
in a World of Uncertainty
Greg Laurie
ISBN 08307.38312

Available at Bookstores Everywhere!

Visit **www.regalbooks.com** to join **Regal's FREE e-newsletter.**
You'll get useful **excerpts from our newest releases** and **special access to online chats with your favorite authors.** Sign up today!

Regal
God's Word for Your World™
www.regalbooks.com

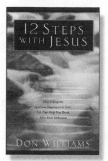
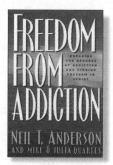